Existential Therapy

Existential Therapy: Distinctive Features offers an introduction to what is distinctive about this increasingly popular method. Written by two practising existential psychotherapists, with many years' experience, it provides an accessible, bitesize overview of this psychological therapy. Using the popular Distinctive Features format, this book describes 15 theoretical features and 15 practical techniques of existential therapy.

Existential Therapy will be a valuable source for psychotherapists, clinical, health and counselling psychologists, counsellors, psychiatrists, and all who wish to know more about the existential approach.

Professor Emmy van Deurzen is an authority on existential therapy with a worldwide reputation. She has published 16 books in the field and is the founder of the Society for Existential Analysis, and of the New School of Psychotherapy and Counselling at the Existential Academy.

Dr Claire Arnold-Baker is an existential therapist, counselling psychologist and perinatal specialist. She is the DCPsych Programme Leader at NSPC, a joint programme with Middlesex University, where she also teaches and supervises. Claire also regularly runs an Introduction to Existential Therapy workshop.

Psychotherapy and Counselling Distinctive Features

Series Editor: Windy Dryden

The Psychotherapy and Counselling Distinctive Features series provides readers with an introduction to the distinctive theoretical and practical features of various therapeutic approaches from leading practitioners in their field.

Each book in this series focuses on one particular approach and guides the reader through 30 features – both theoretical and practical – that are particularly distinctive of that approach. Written for practitioners by practitioners, this series will also be of interest to trainees, social workers and many others outside the therapeutic tradition.

Titles in the series:

Pluralistic Therapy by John McLeod

Cognitive Analytic Therapy by Claire Corbridge, Laura Brummer and Philippa Coid

Existential Therapy by Emmy van Deurzen and Claire Arnold-Baker

For further information about this series please visit:
https://www.routledge.com/Psychotherapy-and-Counselling-Distinctive-Features/book-series/PCDF

Existential Therapy

Distinctive Features

Emmy van Deurzen and
Claire Arnold-Baker

Routledge
Taylor & Francis Group
LONDON AND NEW YORK

First published 2018
by Routledge
2 Park Square, Milton Park, Abingdon, Oxon OX14 4RN

and by Routledge
711 Third Avenue, New York, NY 10017

Routledge is an imprint of the Taylor & Francis Group, an informa business

British Library Cataloguing in Publication Data
A catalogue record for this book is available from the British Library

Library of Congress Cataloging in Publication Data
Names: Van Deurzen, Emmy, author.
Title: Existential therapy : distinctive features / Emmy van Deurzen and Claire Arnold-Baker.
Description: Milton Park, Abingdon, Oxon ; New York, NY : Routledge, 2018. | Includes bibliographical references and index.
Identifiers: LCCN 2017059157| ISBN 9781138687097 (hbk) | ISBN 9781138687103 (pbk) | ISBN 9781315461939 (ebook) | ISBN 9781315461922 (web) | ISBN 9781315461915 (epub) | ISBN 9781315461908 (mobipocket)
Subjects: LCSH: Existential psychotherapy.
Classification: LCC RC489.E93 V363 2018 | DDC 616.89/14—dc23
LC record available at https://lccn.loc.gov/2017059157

ISBN: 978-1-138-68709-7 (hbk)
ISBN: 978-1-138-68710-3 (pbk)
ISBN: 978-1-315-46193-9 (ebk)

Typeset in Times New Roman
by Keystroke, Neville Lodge, Tettenhall, Wolverhampton

This book is dedicated to the future generations

Daisy, Otto, Ben and Sasha

Contents

List of figures ix
List of abbreviations xi

Introduction 1

Part 1 THEORETICAL FEATURES **3**

1 A philosophical rather than a psychological approach to therapy 5
2 Existential philosophy offers an understanding of what it is like to be human 11
3 Creating a broader perspective on *being-in-the-world* 15
4 Recognising the way in which we relate to others 19
5 The effect of time and temporality on our existence 23
6 Intentionality: Understanding the intentional nature of our actions and reactions 27
7 Focusing on freedom, choice and responsibility 33
8 Death, anxiety and Angst 37
9 Existential guilt 41

10 Paradox and the tension of existence 45
11 Notion of the dynamic self 49
12 Authenticity and inauthenticity 53
13 Finding purpose and meaning: The original project 57
14 Values and human worth 61
15 A well-lived life 65

Part 2 PRACTICAL FEATURES **69**
16 Developing a phenomenological attitude 71
17 The quality of the therapeutic relationship: *I-Thou* 75
18 A descriptive exploration 79
19 Taking stock and being aware of the limitations of life 83
20 Getting the bigger picture: Four dimensions of existence 87
21 Living in the world physically 91
22 Living in the world socially 95
23 Living in the world personally 99
24 Living in the world spiritually 103
25 The emotional world of the client 107
26 Embodiment 113
27 Examining the paradoxes of life 117
28 Revisiting values and beliefs 121
29 Making meaning and discovering purpose 125
30 Finding freedom 131

References 135
Index 141

Figures

5.1	Dialectic of time (DoT)	26
6.1	The process of intentionality	31
20.1	Four dimensions of existence	90
25.1	Emotional compass	109

Abbreviations

BPS	British Psychological Society
CBT	Cognitive Behavioural Therapy
CREST	Centre for Research in Social and Psychological Transformation
DoT	Dialectic of time
DSM	Diagnostic and Statistical Manual
ERA	Existential Research Academy
ICD	International Classification of Diseases
NHS	National Health Service

Introduction

The past decades have seen a burgeoning of the existential approach to therapy, worldwide. Previously the approach had always remained rather obscure and mysterious. It had evolved for over a century through the work of practitioners and psychiatrists such as Binswanger, Boss, Frankl and May, who applied existential philosophical ideas to psychotherapy on an individual basis. However, in the 1980s and 1990s this changed, notably with the work of Irvin Yalom in the USA, but also through the work of Emmy van Deurzen in the UK. Existential therapy training programmes began developing and then started spreading across the globe. There are now 136 worldwide existential therapy institutions (Correia et al., 2016), which stands testament to the truly international reach of the approach. The appeal of the existential approach is that it is direct and that it addresses people's difficulties in living without pathologising them. It focuses on how we exist as human beings and it therefore transcends culture, society, politics and religion.

Although the existential approach does not have the same impact in health services as more mainstream approaches such as CBT, it does form one of the key modalities for counselling psychology trainings in the UK that are part of the BPS. More recently, research centres such as CREST at Roehampton University and ERA at the

Existential Academy have begun conducting research to demonstrate the effectiveness and applicability of the existential approach, thus providing the evidence base for practice.

In today's global village, the world can appear smaller as we become more connected to each other by the virtual media. The paradox that we face as individuals today is that this increase in connectivity, particularly online, can leave people feeling isolated and withdrawn. The existential approach, with its focus on meaning, values and beliefs, provides a good antidote to the *existential vacuum* (Frankl, 1967) that technology can create. Increasingly clients and indeed practitioners from other modalities are turning towards the existential approach for inspiration. Existential ideas offer a way to reconnect to the world around us, to other people and to ourselves in a more meaningful and purposeful manner.

The distinctive features of the existential approach will be explored in this book in such a way that they can be easily applied to other methods. The first part will highlight the philosophical and theoretical aspects of the approach. The second part will focus on the practical implications of existential practice. In life we have to accept the limitations that we come up against, accepting them but also learning from them. In the same way, this book is limited in its scope in terms of its size and for an in depth understanding you will need to supplement your reading with other texts. However, despite this we hope that this slim volume will provide the reader with a good introduction and starting position for further exploration into the approach. We hope you will find it helpful, clear and to the point.

Part 1

THEORETICAL FEATURES

1

A philosophical rather than a psychological approach to therapy

The aspect that most distinguishes existential therapy from all other forms of psychotherapy is that it is a philosophical rather than just a psychological approach to working with people. Before psychology as a discipline came into existence well over a century ago now, people looked to philosophy to help them understand and think about their lives. Of course, psychology has added a lot of insights and provided a lot of factual information that is invaluable to therapists, but it can also alienate them from digging that little bit deeper to connect with people's existential concerns and issues.

Taking a philosophical approach means that existential therapists are concerned with the way in which people live, experience, imagine and think about their lives. Existential therapy takes a holistic view, seeing the individual as part of a wider world and as intrinsically connected with the other people around them. Existential therapists pay attention to the cultural and social and political background a person takes for granted and considers the physical and emotional climate and environment that surrounds them. In contrast, psychological approaches tend to focus more directly on the individual's psyche or self. Psychoanalytic or psychodynamic approaches, for example, focus on the individual's internal drives or forces, often thought to be unconscious, that propel the individual into behaving and acting in a certain manner. They also put considerable emphasis on the person's past experiences. Humanistic and person-centred approaches value the relationship that develops between client and therapist in the here and now. Central to this approach is the belief that a congruent and transparent relationship where the therapist is able to give the client unconditional positive regard will enable the client to work through the difficult feelings or relationships that they have. Cognitive behavioural therapies are concerned with how to modify an individual's thinking or behaving so that they can alleviate the individual's difficulties and set them on a better and more realistic path. Each approach has a particular worldview and focus and therefore creates a particular kind of understanding of what causes distress in individuals and how best to help clients overcome their difficulties. In psychological approaches the cause of this distress is usually seen as lying within the individual. Existential therapy is different in all these respects. Its philosophical approach allows it to explore the client's distress as being evidence of their problems in living. It will explore all the aspects that matter, including past, present and future or the way the person is located in time. It will combine different methods, depending on the explorations that are pertinent at any moment. It will follow the client's lead and encourage a joint exploration whilst seeking to progress in the direction that is most meaningful to the client.

Philosophical enquiry

The philosophical aspects of existential therapy are therefore central. In some sense the therapy is a philosophical enquiry, which is posing questions about the world and investigating many possible answers. In some cases, these questions will not lead to answers but to new and better questions. Some of these questions can be quite abstract in nature as they seek to uncover an aspect of universality about human nature or the world. But most of the time these questions are also deeply personal and are about how a particular person is experiencing these aspects of human reality. Philosophy is strong in method and therefore employs particular ways of thinking and unravelling. Philosophical exploration always encourages a sense of awe about the world and wonderment about what we encounter. Philosophers embark on a process of questioning and challenging, taking nothing for granted. As Socrates (469–399 BCE) famously stated, 'wisdom begins in wonder', and he took the view that 'the unreflective life is not worth living'. A questioning attitude to the world and human existence allows us to think deeply about what is important to us, and how to gain insight into our lives and our world. Philosophers seek to look behind the structures that we impose on our thinking, and encourage us to set out once again on a path of discovery, in search of truth.

The value of truth

Philosophical enquiry demands openness to the subject matter and a systematic exploration that seeks to uncover the underlying principles or essences. We have to start from the assumption that everything is in question and that we begin from a position of doubt. Much of our lives may be built on prejudice and mistaken assumptions. To find true values to live by we have to be prepared to start reconsidering what is true and what is false. Plato expressed the idea that 'Truth is its own reward', and Confucius said: 'The object of the superior man is truth'. For all these philosophers the search for truth was important, as it meant seeking something that was authentic and valid for each situation or fundamental to each object and experience. Seeking truth means trying to get to the core of the experience in as open a way as possible, not clouded by judgements, assumptions or interpretations.

The pursuit of knowledge

A common theme of the ancient philosophers was their focus on knowledge. This pursuit of knowledge was connected to questioning and truth, as they believed that we need to be aware of the limitations of our knowledge. Socrates believed that 'True knowledge exists in knowing that you know nothing', and Confucius stated that 'to know what you know and what you do not know, that is true knowledge'. Knowing what we don't know allows us to see the great wealth of knowledge and understanding available, more than we can possibly grasp. Our own attempts at seeking knowledge will always be set in perspective with the overall quest for truth, so that we are humble in the knowledge that we acquire and open to question what we know so that we can learn something new.

A well-lived life

Philosophers throughout the ages have questioned all aspects of our way of living and our knowledge, but those that are most relevant to existential therapists are those that have concerned themselves with the existence of human beings. Whilst existential philosophers will be examined in greater detail in the next chapter, some of the thinking of the ancient philosophers is still very relevant to our way of living today. For Socrates, Plato, Aristotle and Confucius the pursuit of virtue was paramount to living a good life. Plato observed that 'the greatest wealth is to live content with little'. Aristotle and Heraclites were more concerned with how our actions determined who we are. Heraclites stated: 'The content of your character is your choice. Day by day, what you choose, what you think and what you do is who you become.' These philosophers examined how we think about ourselves, what is important for us and what is the best way of living. There is a long line of classical philosophers, including the Stoics, who each emphasised a different aspect of how to live a good life. These are also things that existential therapists address with their clients.

Philosophy as a way to listen

Philosophy, therefore, lends existential therapists a particular lens through which to approach our lives and those of our clients. This lens fosters an open attitude to what we meet, an openness to all possibilities and all different worldviews. It also focuses our responses to life, from an acceptance of the nature of things to a questioning stance. The philosophical lens also provides us as therapists with a certain way of listening to our clients. We listen for the struggles our clients have in living, how they live their lives and their relationships, the choices they make and the values they hold, rather than listening for psychological disturbance. Existential therapists will also engage in Socratic dialogue to help clients to vocalise their values and to question their lives and way of living, in order that they might find some wisdom and set out on their own path towards truth.

2

Existential philosophy offers an understanding of what it is like to be human

Which philosophy?

The field of philosophy, or the love of wisdom, as a discipline is wide and far reaching and considers many aspects of human existence such as knowledge, morals, ethics, religion, aesthetics and metaphysics. Philosophy provides insights by thinking critically about a range of issues that are of concern to us as human beings. However, the most pertinent philosophical contributions for existential therapists come from those philosophers who focus on human existence, the existential philosophers.

Existential philosophy focuses on understanding human existence, *being* in general and also on the specific way in which humans live and exist in the world. Early existential thinking can be found in the works of Athenian philosophers such as Socrates, Plato and Aristotle. However, it wasn't until the start of the 20th century, with the work of Kierkegaard, the founding father of existentialism, that existential philosophy blossomed on the European continent. This period also marked a significant change in focus towards the human sciences and the development of psychology and psychological therapies.

Existential philosophers

The four main existential philosophers that have inspired therapists are Søren Kierkegaard (1813–1855), Friedrich Nietzsche (1844–1900), Martin Heidegger (1889–1976) and Jean-Paul Sartre (1905–1980). However, existential therapists will also draw on the works of other existential philosophers such as phenomenologist Edmund Husserl (1859–1938), theologian Martin Buber (1878–1965), Karl Jaspers (1883–1969), Paul Tillich (1886–1965), Simone de Beauvoir (1908–1986), Maurice Merleau-Ponty (1908–1961) and Albert Camus (1913–1960), to name but a few. Existential literature can also be very inspirational and novels by people like Dostoyevsky, Tolstoy, Kafka, Sartre, Camus and de Beauvoir are a good way to become familiar with existential concepts.

All of these authors were interested in examining human existence and their ways of *being in the world*, i.e. the *being* of human beings. They looked at the fundamental aspects of human existence that we all share (ontology), although each philosopher had their own particular focus on the aspect of living they were interested in. This means there is no one model to draw on, no blueprint for living (Deurzen, 1988). Instead, existential philosophy gives us a way, a method, for looking at human existence and the world and is based on certain philosophical assumptions:

- We are part of a world, a universe, which is much greater than ourselves.
- We find ourselves in (*thrown* into) a physical world over which we have little control.
- The world contains certain givens which we cannot change, i.e. our genetics, family, culture, society, geography, the laws of physics.
- We are always in this world with other people and in relation with these others.
- It is in being in relation to others that we define ourselves.
- We have particular ways of making sense of things, through language and ideas.
- We are always in search of purpose and meaning.

Existential philosophy

These philosophical assumptions provide the foundation on which we can understand our relationship to ourselves, others and the world around us. Existential philosophers, however, also examined other fundamental elements of our existence. Warnock (1970) believed the defining element that united existential philosophers was their focus on human freedom. What made the existential philosophers different from those philosophers who had gone before them was the fact that their philosophy had a practical aspect to it. Existential philosophers wanted people to be aware of what Tarnas called 'the most fundamental, naked concerns of human existence' (Tarnas, 1991: 389). Instead of just contemplating freedom from a theoretical perspective, existential philosophers wanted people to experience it and find meaning in it.

Existential philosophers highlighted that the only certainty we have is that we are limited in time, although the exact timing of our death is unknown to us, and this fact causes us to feel anxiety. We are also free rather than, or in addition to, being determined, both in how we make choices in the here and now regarding our values and how we decide to live and therefore define ourselves. Sartre (1943) believed we begin as nothingness and our sense of self is created through our interactions with the world and others: we are a process of becoming.

Our freedom to choose also means that we are responsible for our choices and we have to choose even though there is no way of knowing how these choices will play out in the future; this again causes us to feel anxiety. The absurdity of our existence as highlighted by Camus (1942) means that our existence and our responsibility for it are a struggle we have to grapple with, and it is through this struggle that meaning can be created. Camus concluded that it was this very search for meaning despite, and perhaps even because of, the fundamental absurdity that made life worthwhile.

How to live

Existential philosophers encourage us to confront the reality of our existence and to experience that reality, however anxiety provoking it may be. This confrontation with existence is not intended to paralyse or freeze the individual into inaction due to anxiety and worry but rather to help us to consider how to live better. For Kierkegaard (1843a) the purpose was to live life without illusion in a way that was true to the individual in relation to the infinite. Nietzsche (1895) also put responsibility back on the individual with his notion of the will to power, which motivates us. Nietzsche recognised that human beings sought to gain mastery of their environment and of themselves and that the power to change, or to live, was what inspired us to become who we are capable of being, rather than us being defined by an external being, such as a God. Heidegger (1927) wanted individuals to become aware of their *being* and to take awareness of the way they existed. This could only occur when we recognised our limitations, and particularly the ending of our life in death, and this required us to free ourselves from the impact of others on us. Heidegger believed that through awareness of the reality of our existence we would be able to make better and more authentic choices for ourselves as individuals as to how to live our lives. Sartre (1943) recognised the ways in which people deny the reality of their existence, by deceiving themselves about both what is the case and what is not the case. The fact of our essential nothingness forces us to create ourselves anew all the time and the fact of our freedom forces us to become responsible for our choices. Sartre exposed the human tendency to deny or evade the anxiety or Angst generated by this, by living in *bad faith*, denying reality and not facing up to our limitations.

All these philosophers highlighted how awareness of our existence is difficult to experience but is essential if we are to be true to ourselves. The more we have the courage to face our existence and the anxiety that it produces, the stronger we shall get and the better we shall become at living in a more aware and considered way.

3

Creating a broader perspective on *being-in-the-world*

Existential therapy – a holistic view

A distinctive feature of existential therapy is to view each individual as part of a wider world. The medical model, with its diagnostic classification system (DSM or ICD), tends to reduce individuals to the sum of their presenting issues, highlighting symptoms and signs and ultimately offering a possible label or diagnosis to the client. However, the existential approach sees individuals in terms of their whole existence, their actions and their relationships. This includes the way they relate to their physical environment, to other people, to themselves and to the ideas and meanings that give significance to their world. This view of human beings stems from the phenomenological work of Edmund Husserl (1900) and was elaborated by Martin Heidegger (1927) and Jean Paul Sartre (1943) and other philosophers. Subsequently, existential therapists and psychiatrists – Binswanger (1946), Boss (1963), May et al. (1946), Laing (1959) and Deurzen (2010) – have adapted these philosophical ideas to working with people therapeutically.

Philosophical underpinnings

Being-there

Edmund Husserl created a new method for understanding human consciousness when he established the scientific method of phenomenology. This was intended to approach human existence in a combined objective and subjective manner. A number of existential philosophers have considered more specifically how human beings are always connected to a world and can never have consciousness without this connection. Merleau-Ponty (1962) was particularly interested in exploring our bodily connection with the world and described in detail how our experience is always an embodied one. However, it was Martin Heidegger, whose project was to elucidate the nature of human *being*, who was the first to describe the many connections between individuals and their world. Heidegger (1927) began his examination of human *being* by considering the fundamental aspects that constitute *Being* in general. Heidegger devised the term *Dasein*, which he used to refer to the *being* of human beings. Heidegger's term *Dasein* literally means '*being-there*' and therefore by using this term Heidegger described an essential aspect of human beings: that we have a spatial dimension to our existence. Warnock clarifies this by saying 'we cannot consider a human being except as a being in the midst of a world' (Warnock, 1970: 50). This is an important concept as it suggests that human beings are never isolated beings but are always situated 'there', in the world of a particular existence and of specific relationships; Heidegger states: 'but since inner *worldly* beings are also in space, their spatiality has an ontological connection with the world' (Heidegger, 1996: 102). The word 'there' locates us spatially within a world; we are there, in the middle of a specific world.

Being-in-the-world

Heidegger develops this idea to show that *Dasein* is not just spatially in the world as an object but there is a special quality to the relationship between *Dasein* and the world. Heidegger terms this relationship as *being-in-the-world*. The hyphens which connect the words highlight the connectedness of the individual to a wider context. Heidegger stresses that the compound nature of this term, *being-in-the-world*, demonstrates a 'unified phenomenon' (Heidegger, 1996: 53). *Being-in-the-world* has to be seen as a whole and therefore *Dasein* can only be viewed within the context of being *in* a world. However, *Dasein* is not just *in* the world as a separate entity; Heidegger states: 'There is no such thing as the "being next to each other" of a being called "Dasein" with another being called "world"' (Heidegger, 1996: 55). *Dasein* is part of the world and the world is part of *Dasein*. *Being-in-the-world* is the ground on which *Dasein* understands itself and its interactions. People are part of a world and that world is an intrinsic aspect of their being.

Care or concern

Heidegger examined the various ways in which *Dasein* can be in the world and recognised that all the possible ways, such as

> *to have to do with something, to produce, order and take care of something, to use something, to give something up and let it get lost, to undertake, to accomplish, to find out, to ask about, to observe, to speak about, to determine*
>
> (Heidegger, 1996: 57)

were examples of *taking care*. Heidegger believed that even deficient modes of being-in represented an element of taking care, even if in a limited or rejecting way. Heidegger believed that care or concern (*Sorge*) was an essential, or ontological, aspect of *Dasein* and as the world and *Dasein* are so interconnected that one cannot be viewed without the other, it follows that our relationship to the world is one of care or concern. We are a part of the world and the world is part of us, and therefore we care about the world that we live in and the relationships we have; they matter to us.

Thrownness

Another essential aspect of our *being-in-the-world* is that we are connected to a world that existed before we were born, and which will go on existing after our death. Heidegger calls this concept *thrownness*. We are born (thrown) into a world that we have no control over; all elements of this world have already been in existence. Our parents, the environment we find ourselves in, cultural and societal values, will all form part of this world. As *thrownness*, we too become part of this world, in the same way other people are part of the world. Some people speak of the 'givens of human existence' that we find already fully made up when we arrive in the world; these are the things we cannot change.

Our connection to the world through an existential lens

Heidegger's work on *Dasein* and *being-in-the-world* has been influential in creating a new way of understanding human existence, and this is as relevant to philosophers as it is to psychotherapists. When we look at human beings as interconnected with their world, this brings a new perspective on the relational aspect of human beings as well. From this perspective we cannot understand another or indeed ourselves without taking into consideration the wider context, or world, in which we are living. As existential therapists we need to keep in mind that the client does not just bring their own personality and history into the therapy room: they bring in their whole world and all their world relations. Our job as therapists is to help clients understand the complex interactions they have with their world and other people and how they in turn impact the world and how the world impacts them.

4

Recognising the way in which we relate to others

No man is an island

John Donne's words 'No man is an island, Entire of itself, Every man is a piece of the continent, A part of the main' (Donne, 1624) encapsulate the existential perspective on human relationships; nobody is an island; nobody is alone, in isolation; we are always connected to other human beings. In the same way that we cannot be separated from the world that we live in, we also have inseparable relationships with other people, even when they are absent.

Mitsein*:* being-with

As described in the previous chapter, Heidegger sees human *being* as being one of connection; we are connected to the world in an objective way, i.e. connected to objects and the physical environment, but we are also connected to the world of others. An essential characteristic of human beings is *being-with*. Heidegger states: 'The world of *Dasein* is a *with-world.* Being-in is *being-with*-others' (Heidegger, 1996: 119). Therefore, part of what we encounter in the world are beings who are similar to ourselves, other humans, and as *being-with* we are always in relation to these others. Our world is not only our own but also a shared world and therefore our experiences of the world and ourselves are always understood through the perspective of others. As Mulhall states, 'Dasein establishes and maintains its relation to itself in and through its relations with Others, and *vice versa*' (Mulhall, 1996: 67). In summary, we relate to the physical world, to others and to ourselves through these other relationships as well. Even in situations where we are alone, we always know of the existence of others and this impacts on how we understand and experience ourselves in the world.

The-They

As *being-with* we come to understand ourselves in relation to others. However, Heidegger notes that we can either find ourselves or lose ourselves in our relationship with others. For the most part we become subsumed by others in our average everydayness. We are fallen with others, taken over by them, before we learn to see others as other. This fallenness is a deficient mode of being, where we become part of an anonymous 'They'. The-They tell us what we should do. The-They represent society's values and beliefs. However, we are also part of the-They, and the-They are part of us. Only by rising above this anonymous (and ultimately always only imaginary) mass of other people can we make authentic choices for ourselves. Nietzsche (1882) makes a similar observation when he describes herd mentality, where we go along with what others do, and Kierkegaard (1849) also notes that we often become so overwhelmed by acting as an individual that we resort to the safety of the crowd. In other words, we hide in others.

Being-for-others

Sartre also described the human relationship to others. He noted that as human beings we are fundamentally a nothing trying to become a something. We wish to be solid as an object is and we derive our sense of being substantial from the way in which the other regards us. The look of the other makes us into an object, for better or for worse. When Sartre (1943) examined the existence of others, he did this by examining the experience of shame. Sartre noted that we only experience shame in relation to other people, either directly or indirectly, by thinking about how others would see our actions. The other's act of looking at us defines us and thus affects us deeply so that we become changed by this interaction. Sartre gives the example of a man looking through a keyhole. When the man realises he has been discovered in the act, he feels shame. Shame comes from being labelled or understood in a particular way by the other and the man sees himself as an object in the eyes of the other.

Sartre notes that the other, in this way, always has power over us. The other is able to define us and therefore can influence us greatly. When Sartre describes and elucidates the ways in which people relate to each other, he concludes that the nature of human relationships is one of conflict. The conflict arises because we are trying to capture and objectify the other while at the same time attempting to free ourselves from being captured by the other.

I-It *and* I-Thou

There are similarities between Sartre's views on relationships and Buber's (1929) work. Where Sartre spoke of being-in-itself (as an object) and being-for-itself (as subjective consciousness), Buber spoke of all relationships as being either *I-It* or *I-Thou* relationships. Buber, like Sartre, noted that human beings relate in an *I-It* way, when we view the other person as an object. We then relate to the other person in the same way we would relate to an object that we could use in an instrumental way. However, Buber believed that human beings are also able to relate to each other in what he calls an *I-Thou* way. This involves a deep way of relating where each individual reaches out to the other in an open way and seeks to understand the other person as a whole, as a subject. When we do so, we address the totality of the other person, we even see their potential and infinite possibilities, as if they were godlike. During this process, acceptance and understanding are communicated between both individuals in a deep and meaningful way.

Sartre's competition and collaboration

Interestingly, Sartre's ideas evolved in a similar direction. Initially he thought that people always related in a competitive mode, because of the conflict between them. He thought this meant either we could try to dominate, or submit, or else we could feign indifference to the other. But later on he came to grasp that we can also relate to others in a collaborative mode, where we discover that by giving to each other we can establish cooperative and reciprocal relationships that benefit us all and that lead to mutuality and generosity. This wider and more positive view of relationship was much influenced by Simone de Beauvoir's work.

An existential perspective on human relationships

Existential philosophy highlights the complexity of our human relationships with others. All the existential authors demonstrated the importance of others in our lives and how others have an impact on us and vice versa. However, this impact can often lead to deficient ways of relating that are not always beneficial to us as individuals. The paradoxical nature of relationships is that we find ourselves between two poles of existence, living life either in an individualistic way or by being part of a group. The challenge we face as human beings is finding our own way to be with others whilst becoming more individual at the same time. We need to find our freedom to be an individual without isolating ourselves relationally on the one hand and to relate and coexist with others without being subsumed by them on the other hand. It is another paradox of life that the better we become at truly loving others, then the better we become at being alone as well.

5

The effect of time and temporality on our existence

Time

Time is important to us as human beings because we are limited in time. Our existence has a finite length, although we do not know how long our life will be. We are bounded by time and so time is intrinsically tied to our experience of being as a boundary marker. Time is also a relative or abstract concept as Albert Einstein (1961) demonstrated with his theory of relativity. We use clock time as a measure, but our experience of time is subjective; time can feel like it is speeding up or slowing down depending on our experience and what we are doing. Ellenberger observed this when he wrote that 'time is experienced as flowing with a certain *speed*' (Ellenberger, 1958: 103).

Heidegger highlighted the importance of time when examining human existence in his book *Being and Time* (1927). He noted that we are always living *in* time as our existence will end with our death. He was interested in how we live in time and how we live with the possibility of our own death and how that affects our existence. Heidegger's view on death will be discussed further in Chapter 8. For Heidegger, time is also linked to his concept of authenticity, as we must choose how to spend our hours. Authenticity will be explored later in Chapter 12. As we can see, time is a complex concept that links our experience of life to the possibility of our death and that deeply affects the choices we make.

Temporality

A few existential authors have written specifically about time and temporality (Heidegger, 1927; Minkowski, 1933; Binswanger, 1946). They all distinguish between the experience of time and lived time. Lived time is described as 'the real inner time-happening' and experienced time is the 'objectified, thought time' (Binswanger, 1946: 301). Heidegger terms lived time as *within-time-ness*, our internal experience of time, our experience of how 'present things come into being and pass away' (Heidegger, 1996: 306).

Lived time also relates to our experience of the past, present and future. Traditionally temporality is viewed as being a straight line, on a past–future axis. However, existential authors have questioned this and suggest that temporality is more circular in our experience than just a sequence of events. In addition, they consider how our experience of time relates to our experience of timelessness or eternity. Heidegger (1996) talks about the three *ec-stasies* of time: 1. being-ahead-of-oneself (future), 2. having-been (past) and 3. being-with (present). These are joined together to form the life cycle of existence and, therefore, every moment of *being* contains within it the past, present and future.

Heidegger understands our existence as projected thrownness, in that we are always orientated to the future and project ourselves into the future. During that process, we will have a present and a past: 'Temporality temporalizes itself as a future which makes present in a process of having been' (Heidegger, 1962: 401).

As mentioned in Chapter 3, Heidegger believed that *Dasein* exists as care and it is temporality that gives care its meaning. Care is the way in which we go out of ourselves into the world and connect to it and this always happens in the context of our project towards a future. We care because we are empty and in movement towards a future which will fulfil us. We are limited in time and thus temporality gives our existence meaning and purpose. It is temporality that makes the unity of our existence possible. Mulhall explains Heidegger's position like this:

> *If Dasein's capacity to relate itself to Being (its own and that of any other being) is of its essence, and if that essence is grounded in its relation to time, then any proper answer to the question of the meaning of Being will inevitably relate Being to time.*
>
> (Mulhall, 1996: 145)

Minkowski further analysed our temporal nature by looking at time as zones of experience. He noted that: the remote past is the zone of the obsolete, the mediate past is the zone of the regretted, the immediate past is the zone of remorse, the immediate future is the zone of expectation and activity, the mediate future is the zone of wish and hope, and the remote future is the zone of prayer and ethical action (Minkowski, 1933: 106). Of course, we are involved in all of these projects at once.

Working with time

Looking at how we live in time can help us understand our existence. Do we talk about having no time? Or do we feel that we are wasting time? How we live in time will give us a focus and a purpose and it will connect our lives to its objectives in a way that creates meaning.

Considering temporality from a Heideggerian perspective can help us understand how we think about things that have happened in the past or might happen in the future. Although our past experiences cannot be changed, our recollection of these experiences or events may differ depending on our present experience. Therefore, the present moment affects our past. Our past experiences will also affect how we are feeling in the present as they provide a reference point from which we can learn. The future is also contained within our present as we are always projecting ourselves into the future. Our future aspirations will also affect actions in the present. Our past experiences can also affect how we think about the future and what we feel might be possible. However, our future aspirations can make us think differently about our past. We are constantly connecting with our past, present and future in an expanding spiral towards eternity. If we focus too much on one aspect of temporality, such as our past, then we have a one-dimensional view. We may get locked in a loop that keeps us going over the past, or worrying about an uncertain future all the time. Some people believe that being in the present, focusing on the here and now, fixes this preoccupation with past or future. But the existential perspective on time is that the more we are able to dynamically move between past, present, future and infinity, the more dialectical our life will be. This view of temporality is illustrated in Figure 5.1 and shows the complexity of temporality and the connections and interactions between all of its aspects. Our present experience affects both past and future and is in turn affected by how we integrate both. Getting awareness of the way we live in time gives us enormous freedom and brings the capacity to dialectically overcome a tendency to remain caught in a particular moment.

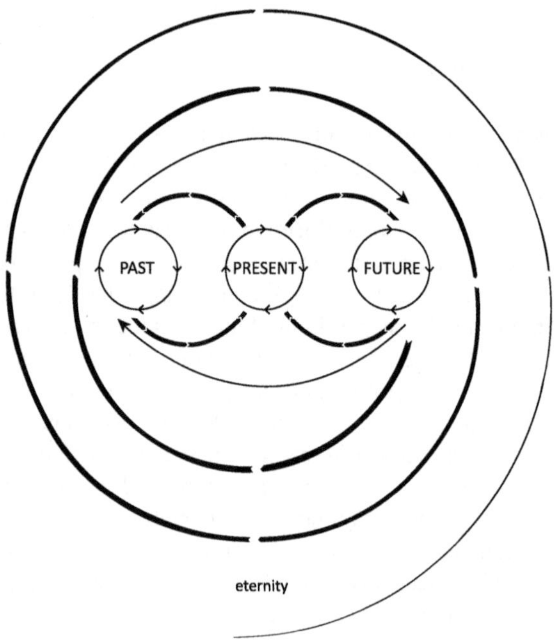

Figure 5.1 Dialectic of time (DoT)

6

Intentionality

Understanding the intentional nature of our actions and reactions

In previous chapters, we have highlighted the connected and relational nature of human beings. Another important aspect of this connectivity is that we are intentional beings. The idea of intentionality allows us to understand and describe how we act and interact in the world, but also how we experience and reflect on the world. Everything we think, feel and do is related to something outside of us. Our actions and reactions always happen in response to something and they are always purposeful. Human existence never takes place in a vacuum. We are not in isolation but always connected, and our lives are always situated within a context. Everything has a subject, an object and a direction of movement and change.

Franz Brentano

It was Franz Brentano (1874) who reintroduced the concept of intentionality to describe the relationship between our mental acts and the external world. Brentano observed that every psychological act or mental phenomenon was directed towards an object. There is an intentional arc that connects us to the object of what we see, do or want. Our desires always involve a desired object or objective. However, these objects do not have to be concrete objects; they don't have to exist in reality, as they can be actions or ideas instead. For example, we can be afraid of flying in an aeroplane without being in an aeroplane. We can laugh about an imaginary future. Therefore, the object of our fear or laughter is a concept of our thinking. Brentano believed that the way in which we presented objects in our mind demonstrated that we are always intentional in our existence. It is therefore important to understand the intentional world in which we live and see how we play a part in constituting it.

Edmund Husserl

Husserl, influenced by Brentano, his teacher, developed the notion of the intentionality of consciousness. He believed that 'all consciousness is consciousness of something'. Husserl described the 'intentional content' of thought. He distinguished between the intentional act, the intentional object and the intentional content in our mind (Husserl, 1900). Certain types of mental activity, such as perceiving, evaluating and remembering, are referred to as intentional acts. The intentional object is the object towards which the intentional act is directed. Husserl believed that intentionality was the relationship between subject and object. The intentional content refers to the way in which we view the intentional object from a particular perspective or standpoint. In his later work, Husserl described how we create meaning through our interactions with the world. Our act of intentionality (noesis) towards the world confers its meaning (noema). We can also take awareness of this process and our own part in it, which reveals our thinking cogito (nous). Husserl proposed various methods that would allow us to question our usual assumptions about the world by suspending our natural attitude and re-examining what was really there. He called this 'going to the things themselves' and referred to his methods as 'reductions'. The phenomenological reduction helps us focus on the process of consciousness, the noesis. The eidetic reduction helps us focus on the objects of consciousness, the noemata. The transcendental reduction helps us to get clarity about the subject of consciousness, the transcendental ego, or nous. In this way, we can make better sense of what we are experiencing.

Martin Heidegger

Heidegger (1927) developed Husserl's view of intentionality and gave it a psychological twist. He noted that we always exist in time and therefore are always outside of ourselves, as we are in the process of changing and moving forwards towards the future. This is also a way of directing ourselves towards something with intentionality; we are always in relation to the external world and going towards our own completion of ourselves as we move towards our final moment in death. For Heidegger, we always approach something from a certain stance: from where we find ourselves in the world. Heidegger noted that this meant that our connection to the world is therefore never neutral. As Deurzen explains: 'the world is not a neutral place, but is laden with value in accordance with what I bring near or keep far away from me' (Deurzen, 1997: 36). In directing ourselves towards the world we gain a new perspective on the world and this perspective is always open to change.

Jean-Paul Sartre

Sartre (1943) viewed intentionality from the perspective of our reflective consciousness. He thought that we are only partially aware of our intentionality, i.e. of that which is available for us to reflect on in consciousness. Sartre posited that becoming more aware of our intentionality enables us to redirect ourselves to new things and events and also new ways of being. We can grasp our intentionality in a new way, which allows for our meaning of the world and our experiences, both past and present, to be changed. Sartre spoke about the way we are different when we are just acting towards a goal, being for ourselves, or when we are aware of ourselves in the eyes of others, and being for others. In the latter case, we become self-conscious. We want the approval of others, who can make us feel stronger as they define us almost as if we are an object, so that we become a being in itself. But we also become caught in the other's look and reduced to less than we are capable of being as a being for itself. We feel shame as we fear others disapprove of us and this diminishes us. We have a tense relationship with others for this reason, until we find a way of collaborating, which is when our intentionality dovetails with that of others and we work together for the same values.

Merleau-Ponty

For Merleau-Ponty (1962) intentionality is an embodied experience, as it is through our body that we reach to grasp an object in front of us: 'consciousness is being-towards-the-thing through the intermediary of the body' (Merleau-Ponty, 1962: 138–139). Merleau-Ponty felt there was an ambiguous intertwining between the inner subjective experience and the outer objective experience. He pointed out that there is a continuous ambiguity as the hand with which we touch the world is at the same time the hand the world touches. Human existence is always a way of transforming something that we have been given or that has been done to us. Intentionality is the process by which this transformation is effected. He believed that the body always moves through the world in an intentional way as pre-reflective consciousness but that we can take awareness of this consciousness and therefore bend it in new directions.

The importance of understanding our intentionality

Intentionality flavours the whole of our existence. It gives us the direction and the way in which we approach the world. It always has an emotional flavour as well. Intentionality is the lens through which we perceive the world and experience ourselves. It is our context and how we make sense of the world that creates meaning in our lives. To gain a deeper understanding of how we act in the world, we first have to understand the standpoint we come from, the ground on which we stand, which will include our values and beliefs, our past experiences and our embodiment. If we are able to reflect on our particular vantage point, then we will better understand our intentionality, and the way in which we respond and act in the world. We will also be able to be more purposeful and active in the way in which we reach out to the world and to others and thus in the process gain a new perspective or understanding on life.

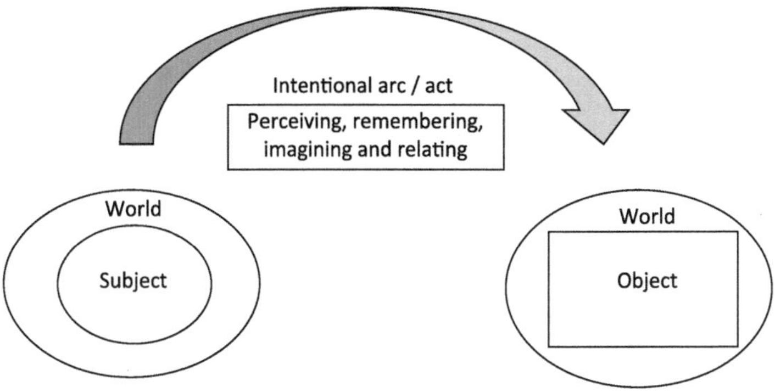

Figure 6.1 The process of intentionality

7

Focusing on freedom, choice and responsibility

Freedom

The question that has generated much debate amongst thinkers since the early Greek philosophers is whether human beings have free will or if we are determined. If our actions are indeed determined by external circumstances, this suggests that for every event there can only ever be one course of action, one particular outcome. Determinism is linked to causal relationships, where we might investigate or try to understand what has caused or led up to an action taking place. Psychology has often focused on investigating cause and effect relationships as a way of trying to understand and simplify the complexity of human relationships. The difficulty we face with determinism is that there is no room for individual choice and there is also no place for the recognition of pluralism and multiple connections between things. It suggests a rather linear way of thinking. If we are to take determinism to its logical conclusion, all actions or events run along predictable chains of causality and thus are more or less predetermined or foretold, and that includes our responses to them.

Choice

We know that people do not experience their own lives in this manner. They are often confused by the many options open to them and by the complexity of the different combinations of choices they can make. The question of freedom or free will therefore becomes a question about these choices. Do we as human beings have a choice in how we respond? For existential philosophers, notably Sartre (1943), the answer is yes, human beings are fundamentally free to choose: free to choose not only how to respond in the next moment but also free to choose ourselves in the way we opt to be and become. For Sartre, our freedom is not something we can choose to exercise or not; we are 'condemned to be free' (Sartre, 1943:553), we have no other option, we *are* free and therefore we *have* to choose. The choices that we must make are not just the big choices in life, i.e. what type of job we would like, or where or with whom we would like to live; rather our life is made up of moment by moment choices that we are often unaware of. Deurzen explains it like this: 'Every move we make, everything we decide, is more plausibly regarded as the outcome of a multitude of influences, which include elements of past, present and future expectations' (Deurzen, 1997: 96). How we spend each moment and how we respond to others and our situation are the choices we must make. While this is often very difficult, these choices are also what makes life interesting. Our freedom to choose also comes out of and is limited by our connection to the external world. We are constantly confronted with our existence in the world around us, and how we navigate this world is determined by the way in which we respond to the context we are in and the events that are happening to us. Sartre stated that we have no choice but to choose. If we do not choose, that is also a choice but this is a choice to live our life passively rather than actively. Effectively we are constantly responding to things that are happening: we are responding to the givens of the world and we do so either deliberately or by default. Perhaps it is more of an interaction between freedom and determination. Some things just are the way they are, but we still can resolve to have one or another response to them.

Merleau-Ponty (1962) examines freedom from the perspective of our embodiment and our perception. For Merleau-Ponty our attitude towards the world influences the way in which we perceive the world. Our attitudes transform the world and we evaluate objects in terms of how they affect us. If we meet the world with anger, we shall encounter an angry world, which in turn will affect our response to it. However, the world also transforms us: 'we choose our world and the world chooses us . . . freedom is always a meeting of inner and outer' (Merleau-Ponty, 1962: 454). It is this intertwining of inner and outer, Merleau-Ponty argues, that demonstrates our freedom. Merleau-Ponty referred to this as the ambiguity of existence: we are both products of the world and producers of a new world. We are both created by circumstances and create new ones. De Beauvoir (1948) also wrote about this tension in her book *The Ethics of Ambiguity*.

Responsibility

Sartre's concept of freedom, and therefore choice, is directly linked to responsibility. If we truly are free to choose how to live, to choose how to respond to the events in our lives, both past and present, then we are also responsible for those choices. A deterministic view of existence absolves us from our responsibility; freedom condemns us to it. To be responsible is literally to be answerable. Life poses a question or makes a statement and we respond to it; this is our responsibility: our capacity to take charge of our active response to the world and our ownership of the consequences that our response may lead to.

The life we lead, the person we become, the choices we make, are our responsibility and ours alone. Existential therapists believe that by becoming more aware of our freedom, and the responsibility it holds over us, we can make better choices for ourselves. Rather than blaming our situation on past events or on other people (say our parents) we can take responsibility for our part in what has happened and choose how to live and respond differently in the future. This also means that we are not held back by what has gone before; we can challenge notions of who we think we are and we can choose to live in very different ways. In this sense, we are not just responsible, or answerable, for the present situation we are in, but also for the way in which we understand our past and create a new world for the future. Of course, this idea of being completely free and responsible for ourselves is not as attractive as it first may seem. With choice and responsibility comes anxiety, which we will discuss in the next chapter.

8

Death, anxiety and Angst

Anxiety – the existential paradox of choice

Kierkegaard is best known for his lively descriptions of the concept of anxiety, or Angst, i.e. existential anxiety. This interest in the concept of anxiety was later echoed in the work of both Heidegger and Sartre. For Kierkegaard and Sartre, the existential paradox that we face is that we have to choose; our freedom demands that we do so, but there is no way of knowing how these choices will affect us. We have to make choices blind and it is this aspect of our choice that provokes anxiety. We are constantly fearful of making the wrong decisions. Kierkegaard states that existential paradox, and therefore anxiety, is an essential part of human existence, which we cannot escape from. He highlighted the paradox we face by stating that we can only understand life backwards, by evaluating the choices we have made and making sense of them, but that we must live our life forwards and thus have to take risks. This for Kierkegaard leads to the 'dizziness of freedom' (Kierkegaard, 1844: 61), when we are faced with the unknown infinity of possibilities and have to somehow hold strong and find our courage and make a choice anyhow. Kierkegaard compares this experience to standing by the abyss, because we fear annihilation if we fail in our endeavour. Sartre (1943) explained this with his example of vertigo when standing on a cliff; it is not the height that we fear rather it is what we might choose to do in the next moment that we fear, for we may feel like jumping off the cliff. Everything and anything is possible, including our own actions, but they are unknown to us, until the moment of action and until we can oversee the consequences of that action.

Existential anxiety

Existential anxiety is a particular form of anxiety that comes when we consider our existence and contemplate questions such as 'who am I?' or 'how do I exist?' or 'what is life for?' According to Kierkegaard, another paradox of our existence is that we are held between various tensions: the temporal versus the eternal, the finite versus the infinite and necessity versus possibility. These tensions represent the elements that are contained within our self and also within the universe.

First of all we have to grapple with the fact that we live in time, the temporal, which means that our lives are subject to constant flux; however, we also have to be ourselves – a self that we recognise in relation to something eternal, something that is unchanging, important and universal.

The finite and the infinite refer to what we know and how we feel. It is the tension between acknowledging the facts (finite) as well as the truth (infinite) about our existence and at the same time engaging our freedom to opt for a suitable course of action. Mullen gives an example of this when he says: 'It *is* appropriate, of course, to mourn the loss of a loved one, but not in a way that destroys your own life and the life of others' (Mullen, 1995: 49).

The final dialectical pair is that of necessity and possibility. This pair refers to who I am as an individual and can become. It brings out the tension between the constriction of what is now and all the possibilities that we can imagine, i.e. the multiple ways in which we can choose to live our lives. On the one hand we need to face the necessity of how life actually is and on the other hand we need to give ourselves leeway to change it. These two opposing tensions allow us to be both creative and realistic (Mullen, 1995: 48). Kierkegaard's philosophy demonstrates the paradoxes that we all face: acknowledging the facts whilst being open to the freedom of possibilities. Both need to be present. Who we are is therefore a product of how we choose to live with these tensions. Sometimes we get stuck with a sense of necessity and determination and at other times we are overawed by the wide range of possibilities.

Death anxiety

Another aspect of existential anxiety can be found in Heidegger's philosophy. Heidegger highlighted the impact of our temporal nature, that we are limited in time. The only thing that we can be certain of in life is that we will die; however, the time and manner of our death are unknown to us and it is this that causes us to feel anxiety. This is about facing the end of our possibilities.

Our fear of our own non-being means that we try to distract ourselves from the anxiety it causes. Heidegger describes ways in which in our everyday life we flee from death, distract and tranquillise ourselves from thoughts of our own and others' death. However, Heidegger notes that there are times when we are faced with death in a limited way, by failing, or losing something or someone. At these moments we become aware of our death as a possibility and we move into a 'being towards death' mode of being. In this mode, we are able to see our life as it is, with all its limitations. In this way, we can actually get a sense of our complexity and completeness and own our existence, past, present and future. This needs strength and requires us to face our anxiety, but in doing so we are able to see what is important to us and make choices that are more in line with the life we would like to live. The limit of death provides us with a frame within which to make the most of our existence.

Embracing anxiety

Kierkegaard, Heidegger and Sartre all acknowledge the importance of understanding anxiety in our lives. Deurzen notes that Kierkegaard's insight that anxiety needs to be used as a guide rather than eliminated goes against most modern therapeutic approaches: 'Anxiety indeed should be the starting point of therapy, not in order to alleviate it, but rather because anxiety must be considered the starting point of a well-lived life' (Deurzen, 1997: 13). If we have the courage to examine and understand the anxiety we feel, or the feelings of unsettledness it brings, we can gain a better sense of how we might live in a more active way in line with what is important for us. As Kierkegaard said, ‘whoever has learnt to live with anxiety, has learnt the ultimate’.

9

Existential guilt

As the previous chapter showed, existential anxiety is an intrinsic part of our existence. It is our response to the complex challenges of existence, a response to the reality of our freedom and the fact that we are limited in time. It infuses us with the energy required to face these challenges. Existential guilt is the counterpart to existential anxiety and relates not to the fact that we need to make choices, but rather to the nature of these choices and our attitude towards them.

When we view human existence as providing us with freedom, this commits us to having to create ourselves and our lives by making choices. We do this consciously by taking into account all the possibilities that are available to us in our imagination and balancing them against the reality of our lives. As Sartre (1943) highlighted, we have no choice but to choose. Not choosing is also a choice. However, we are presented with many possibilities from which to choose and so our freedom also means that there are always possibilities that we have to reject. Choosing always requires a rejection of something; even trying to sit on the fence and not making a decision is a choice of rejecting all our options.

Heidegger (1927) showed that as thrownness we are always behind on ourselves, as the world already exists before we are part of it and therefore the possibilities available to us are already there to be chosen. How we choose will depend on our position or view towards the world and our mode of being. Heidegger describes two modes of being that we can opt for, an authentic and an inauthentic mode, and these will be discussed further in Chapter 12. Essentially, Heidegger argued that for the most part we get lost in living an anonymous type of life, going along with the flow, following other people's expectations and those of society. In this inauthentic way, we lose our capacity for making choices as the possible ways of living have already been chosen for us. We live the anonymous life of doing what we think others expect of us. The advantage of going with the flow is that we avoid the anxiety of having to choose ourselves, we avoid the nausea (Sartre, 1938) of being confronted with the fear of emptiness and nothingness.

Heidegger (1927) noted that when we become conscious of ourselves and our existence, through our experiences of existential anxiety or death anxiety, we also experience guilt. This guilt is not like neurotic guilt, i.e. feeling guilty about doing something wrong, which is connected to moral guilt. Instead, existential guilt is linked to our sense of who we are and how we are being. Heidegger refers to it as 'being guilty'. Being guilty for Heidegger is being indebted to ourselves. Being responsible for who we are means we owe ourselves something. Heidegger sees this indebtedness as a lack, something that is missing or not present in our existence. Heidegger argues that guilt does not arise from the lack, but is part of it. Indeed, experiencing a lack is what it means to be human and this inevitably means that we are guilty. Existential guilt highlights the things that we are lacking. Existential guilt discloses the fact that we have not made choices for ourselves as individuals but have accepted choices that have been presented to us by others and society on what we ought to do.

Existential guilt, therefore, prompts us to look again at our lives and ourselves. We experience an uncomfortable feeling, an unsettledness, a feeling that all is not right, which Heidegger calls being *unheimlich*, i.e. being unsettled or not at home with ourselves. It is this unsettled feeling that makes us more aware and pushes us to think about our lives. Heidegger takes the view that being human is always to feel ill at ease and not at home in some way. Often clients will come to therapy stating that they don't know what is wrong, but they just feel out of sorts with life. This experience is the *call of conscience* (Heidegger, 1927). This call does not tell us what choices to make, only that we need to make a choice. The call wakes us up from the stupor of our life and gives us an opportunity to think about ourselves and how we are living. It is in these moments when we face up to the realities and limits of our existence that we can make authentic choices for ourselves as individuals, to live in the best possible way and to be the best possible version of ourselves. Of course, this might not always be possible, and people may still choose to stay in difficult relationships or unsatisfying jobs even after experiencing existential guilt. But the important thing is that these are choices that are made actively, that the individual has thought through all the possibilities that are available and then made a choice, even if it is to remain the same. This is what existential guilt is calling us to do, to take ourselves seriously and to act, to make a choice, to think deeply about our lives and not to choose passively. Guilt is what makes us thoughtful and therefore capable of authentic living.

10

Paradox and the tension of existence

'I am the wisest man alive, for I know one thing, and that is that I know nothing' (Plato, *The Republic*). In this quote about Socrates, Plato grasps one of the paradoxes of life: that our wisdom is always based in an understanding of our ignorance. We only grow wise when we begin to know what we don't know. Life is ambiguous and contradictory. Everything in life has an opposite and counterpart. All is tension and antinomy. We cannot have a concept of good unless we also have a notion of bad. The opposition helps to define each element of existence. Deurzen elucidates this when she writes: 'The human condition is riddled with contradictions. We live in a constant tension between opposites, moving between wakefulness and sleep, confidence and doubt, belonging and isolation, sickness and health, life and death' (Deurzen, 1998: 1). We cannot have one side of the polarity without the other. Every light casts a shadow and we can only see things because of the contrast. We only get the whole picture of something when we understand the downsides as well as the upsides.

What this means in daily life is that we are constantly caught in the tensions between opposing poles. Kierkegaard, as discussed in Chapter 8, was particularly aware of this in his philosophy. He was dedicated to exploring the paradoxes and contradictions that are inherent in our existence and what this means for ourselves and our humanity. Kierkegaard believed that we should not aim for one side of the polarity at the exclusion of the other. Both are equally present in each moment and equally important. We oscillate between the two, but must hold on to both aspects at the same time and experience that tension. It is the choices that we make whilst existing in the tension that determine our relation to each polarity or paradox we encounter. Merleau-Ponty and Simone de Beauvoir have both spoken about the same thing in terms of ambiguity. Merleau-Ponty spoke of the ambiguity of human existence as always involving both an inside and outside perspective: when we touch we are also touched, we make something of what has been made of us. Similarly, Beauvoir noted the importance of ambiguity in our active and passive roles in life. She showed how many of our experiences can be interpreted in lots of different ways. Deurzen applied this idea to therapy, where we can help people learn to manage this ambiguity and paradox by working creatively with the tensions and contradictions.

Life and death: the ultimate paradox

Probably the greatest paradox that we face as human beings is that of life and death. From the moment that we are born we are faced with the possibility of our demise. We can only truly live to the extent that we are willing to accept our limitations and come to terms with the ultimate limit of our future death. Heidegger argued that life only makes sense in relation to death and only comes into its own when we face up to our mortality. It is death that provides the boundaries to life and in turn gives our life focus and purpose. Yalom (1980) spoke of the way in which death provides the frame within which we can create our human existence.

Indeed, most existential authors have written about death as a defining aspect of our existence (Heidegger, 1927; Jaspers, 1951; Tillich, 1952). All these authors noted that our natural response to the paradox of life and death is to try to avoid or deny death, as it causes us too much anguish (Chapter 8). However, these authors also understood that if we think more openly about death, this can positively affect the way we live life. Heidegger, in particular, believed that we should see death as an ever-present possibility, as we do not know the timing or manner of our death. We die a little bit each day. However, this does not mean viewing death in a morbid manner, as the latter could paralyse us into inactivity. Rather, death brings our life into focus. When we become aware that we are limited in time and that our existence has a boundary, we are able to see our life as a picture that is in the process of being completed, from start to finish. This helps us to make more meaningful choices as we become aware of the urgency of life.

This is also true for other paradoxes and contradictions that we face in life. On every level of our existence, we will be presented with tensions that will challenge us. We may err on the side of caution, aiming towards a more positive or easy side of life, looking to experience joy and trying to avoid suffering, but in doing so our existence becomes one dimensional. We may feel safer or less stressed, but we lose the richness and depth of existence. We can only feel great happiness if we have experienced great sadness. Each time we allow ourselves to feel a loss deeply, we can also appreciate our desire and work towards something we love and truly savour it. We need these opposites to stretch and deepen the frame of our existence. This is no easy task and takes existential courage (Tillich, 1952). Existential therapy is about finding a gentle way to face those aspects of life that are difficult. It's about facing up to life's challenges and allowing both the good and the bad, the joy and the suffering, into our lives.

Existential philosophy highlights this paradoxical nature of existence. An inevitable part of being human is that we will face contradictions, paradoxes and tensions. Philosophy can teach us that when we face these tensions, it is not a case of making an either/or choice, accepting one side of the paradox and rejecting the other. Neither is it a case of finding a compromise. It is about accepting tensions and both sides of the equation and allowing our lives to be transformed by the power of the paradox. The better we understand polarities and where we stand in relation to them, the easier it becomes to master the way we live our lives. This will enable us to experience life to a fuller extent and to live more deeply, aiming to live dialectically, which means that we shall seek to surpass or transcend the opposites, allowing change to happen.

11

Notion of the dynamic self

'Know thyself' was the rallying cry that has often been attributed to Socrates, but it was actually the motto written above the temple of Apollo in Delphi. The question of what this self *is* has preoccupied philosophers throughout history. The self has sometimes been thought of in terms of a kind of personal essence or a soul. However, philosophers such as Locke (1689) and Hume (1739) have been perplexed by how we can be constantly changing, whilst retaining a sense of ourselves. Hume thought of the self as a commonwealth of elements rather than a fixed core; the individual elements could change yet the body it belongs to, i.e. the commonwealth, remains the same. Locke felt that there needed to be psychological continuation, which would require memory, although this too is problematic as we need to be able to account for how our sense of self continues after a deep and dreamless sleep or a period of unconsciousness.

Probably the most defining feature of an existential approach to therapy is its view of the self as a process rather than a thing. This is quite distinct from psychological conceptions which tend to envision the self as something more solid or substantial and which endures over time. Some authors in the psychology and psychotherapy field recognise that the self is a process, yet also want to define it in terms of personality or ego, so that it becomes something that can be measured or categorised. The existential view in contrast is that the self is a continuous process of becoming and transformation: 'Selfhood might be best defined as the dynamic and ever-changing experience of being at the narrative centre of gravity of one's particular world experience' (Deurzen and Arnold-Baker, 2005: 160).

Sartre's view that 'existence precedes essence' (Sartre, 1943) is a defining starting point for our conception of the self in existential therapy. It is based in the observation that we need to live first, through experiencing the world and interacting with others, before we can get an understanding of ourselves. It is the way in which we exist that gives us a sense of who we are. We shape a self out of the things we do and achieve and the way in which other people regard us. We become how we act. We create ourselves by what we connect with and what we do. Although each existential author conceives of the self in slightly different ways, they share this same overarching principle, that the self is a process, an interaction between ourselves and the world in which we live.

Kierkegaard

Kierkegaard (1844), as already described in Chapter 8, took the view that the self is a relation that relates to itself, a synthesis of opposites. These opposing tendencies, the finite and the infinite, the temporal and the eternal and possibility and necessity, are an intrinsic part of human existence and they create tension for us. Rather than having a fixed core which is me, these opposites highlight our freedom, that there are many ways in which we can conceive of ourselves and our lives. However, as mentioned previously, this can also lead to experiences of anxiety and despair. Anxiety comes from opening up and facing the emptiness of our self and is the risk we have to take when engaging with the world. Despair is generated when we give up on ourselves and close down our connection with the world. For Kierkegaard then the self is a creation, a dynamic process that comes into being as we oscillate between the paradoxes of our existence and selfhood and go from opening up to closing off our possibilities and back.

Nietzsche

If Kierkegaard's notion was that the self is created through finding a balance between opposing tensions, Nietzsche took an alternative view and believed the self is a more active creation in the overcoming of tensions. He stated: '*Will a Self* – Active, successful natures act, not according to the dictum "know thyself", but as if there hovered before them the commandment: *will a self* and thou shalt *become* a self' (Nietzsche, 1977: 232). Nietzsche believed we had the power to determine ourselves, based on the notion that we are free beings. Nietzsche's view is that we are not just responding to the world around us, but we actively create, and have the power, to be who we want to be.

Heidegger

Heidegger's (1927) ontological exploration of human beings demonstrated how they developed and changed throughout time; he concluded that we are a process of becoming. Human beings, from a Heideggerian perspective, could be described as openness and possibility (Deurzen and Arnold-Baker, 2005: 162). We are connected to the world and others and we get a sense of who we are when we reflect on our interactions. Heidegger believed we are not fixed beings, but a process of continual change. It is only in the moment of death that we become a fixed entity, a finished product. Heidegger's notion of the self is connected to his theories of authenticity and inauthenticity which will be further explored in Chapter 12.

Sartre

Sartre believed that fundamentally human beings were nothing. They were literally no-thing, not a thing, but pure pre-reflective consciousness. Our sense of self comes from us reaching out to the world and interacting with it. In this process we are also continually changing. Sartre also believed that a sense of self is connected to our freedom, in the same way in which Nietzsche thought that we are able to create and re-create ourselves through the choices that we make. Sometimes we feel most real when we are free, yet we crave the certainty that specific commitments bring. We yearn to have a strong and solid identity, which comes from choosing a specific role and way of being.

Recent longitudinal research (Harris et al., 2016) has demonstrated that there is indeed no stable personality over the lifespan. This confirms an existential view of self that our experiences change us and that we are capable of a wide variety of ways of being, acting and thinking about ourselves. All existential authors recognise the role that freedom and responsibility play in the notion of the self. Our responsibility to ourselves and our lives causes us to experience anxiety and Tillich (1952) believed that therefore we needed the 'courage to be', courage to create a self out of nothingness in the knowledge that we are always limited in our existence and yet are constantly faced with unlimited possibilities and responsibilities.

12

Authenticity and inauthenticity

Authenticity, and its counterpart inauthenticity, are crucial and central concepts in existential philosophy and therapy. These notions address the question: 'what does it *mean* to live one's own life?' (Pollard, 2005: 171). Whilst our freedom paradoxically determines that we have to choose our own life, this does not mean that the choices we make will be good or active ones. Most of us are initially inclined to follow in other people's footsteps and to do what we imagine we have to do. It is this element of learning to think about our own choice making in living that philosophers, such as Heidegger, have considered to be elemental. To become aware that we have a choice of either just do what the world dictates or think for ourselves about it and claim our freedom is to mature into an existentially aware individual. Being authentic is not a simple case of making good or bad choices, it is to be aware of our capacity to make choices and allow ourselves the anxiety, guilt and doubt that are tied into this.

Authenticity is often linked to our sense of being a self. When we think of being authentic, it is often in terms of being real or genuine or true to ourselves. As the previous chapter showed, in actual fact our sense of ourselves is continually changing. We are a process and therefore, in the same way, our authenticity changes and is a process too. Therefore, authenticity is better defined as that possibility of taking awareness of our potentiality for life and death. To live authentically is to live with awareness of existential reality, rather than simply being true to a self.

Heidegger – 'the-They'

Heidegger, through his exploration of human *being*, noted that recognising our freedom and responsibility to choose ourselves causes us to experience anxiety. For most of the time we distract ourselves from experiencing this Angst by immersing ourselves in everyday living. We divert ourselves and become what Heidegger calls 'fallen in with others' (Heidegger, 1927). In this mode of being we become like everyone else, a 'They' self, an anonymous self, that copies what we imagine others expect of us. We might say we become a clone of the standard person. We become 'average', as Kierkegaard would have said. 'The-They' is a term Heidegger uses to describe others as we think of them in an anonymous way, as in 'they would want us to be polite'. Of course we are also part of the-They ourselves. We are part of the-They that other people dread or follow. The idea of the-They determines what we 'should' do; it represents all of us, but also the society and culture we live in. When we act as if we are the-They, we act 'normal'. We then make choices merely based on what we feel we 'should' do or what others would want us to do. We avoid anxiety as we have given up responsibility for making choices for ourselves. We go along with the crowd. But the choices we make are not ones that satisfy us. They are blind choices. We are not living up to our potential or living the best possible version of ourselves. In those moments, we are making inauthentic choices and at some level we feel deeply unhappy about this. People who come for therapy are often in this frame of mind and feel uneasy or dissatisfied with it.

Existential guilt and the call of conscience

There are times when we start to become aware of ourselves and how we are living our lives. As we described in Chapter 9, these are times when we feel existential guilt. We get an unsettled feeling, a feeling that something is not quite right. We feel as if something tells us that we are in the wrong, even though we have not made a mistake. This is what Heidegger terms the 'call of conscience' (Heidegger, 1996: 269). The call of conscience wakes us up from our tranquillity and calls us to take awareness of owing something to life and of having to make a choice of our own. As Heidegger states: 'because Da-sein is lost in the "They", it must first *find* itself. In order to find *itself* at all, it must be "shown" to itself in its possible authenticity' (Heidegger, 1996: 268). The call of conscience does not determine what type of choice to make, only that a choice is needed. A choice for ourselves as individuals is a choice where we become aware of all the possibilities available to us. Heidegger likens the call to a summons – something that we cannot ignore – for it tells us something that we need to understand about ourselves and our existence: it has a disclosing quality. Heidegger argues that it is through the call of conscience that we recognise what is lacking in ourselves and our life and that we are confronted with our existential guilt (Chapter 9). Existential guilt highlights how we have failed to live up to our potential. Accepting our guilt and what is lacking enables us to make choices that are more deliberate and more truly considered.

Being authentic

Although for Heidegger being authentic is about living up to our potential and making choices for ourselves as individuals rather than following the herd, he does not put a value judgement on either mode of existing. He maintains that authenticity and inauthenticity are equally important modes of being. In some ways it is as necessary for us to live in an inauthentic way, particularly if we are to live as part of a society and culture; there will be ways of existing that we will need to adhere to. Sometimes we have to stop thinking and just do what is expected of us. We have to know how to fit in as well as knowing when to stand out. Heidegger acknowledges that the only way a human life can be lived is by taking awareness of always being bounced between authentic and inauthentic ways of being. At times, we reflect authentically (with awareness of the limits of life) and face up to reality. At other times, we follow a trodden track and make do with inauthentic ways of being and conformity. Being aware of these two possibilities only happens if we open ourselves up to our possibilities of being. This is a demanding way of life and requires us to take risks and seek truth.

13

Finding purpose and meaning

The original project

Dwelling on your existence, as has been shown in the previous chapters, can cause you to feel anxiety and guilt. This might give the impression that existential philosophy, and therefore existential therapy, is overly negative in nature. Being aware of our death, our doubts, our failures, our anxiety and guilt, might feel uncomfortable but it also has the effect of making us think about how we live and what is important to us. This can bring great satisfaction and joy. Through this type of reflection and questioning we can create a sense of meaning and find purpose in our lives, because we are making new connections and come to understand what is of importance and what is not. It is only by confronting the reality of our existence and looking into those parts that are uncomfortable that we can find out what really matters to us. Discovering this brings a feeling of taking charge of life.

Heidegger: being-towards-death

As we have seen, this capacity for taking ownership of life is linked to Heidegger's idea of the exploration of death. Heidegger (1927) believed that if we lived life as if death was an ever-present possibility (*being-towards-death*), then we would become more aware of all the possibilities that are around us. He didn't mean that we should think about our own death in a morbid way, or worry about dying. Instead he felt that by reflecting on our death, and taking awareness of its presence in our lives, for instance when things come to an ending, we become more authentic. Focusing on the time we have left is anxiety provoking, as we do not know when our ending might be, but it encourages us to make decisions about how we want to fill our lives or spend our time. Being aware of these possibilities and having an awareness of our temporality – that we are limited in time – allows the things that matter to emerge and stand out. Focusing on what is important to us is one way of creating a meaningful life, for it enables us to connect what we do to that source of meaning. It also brings the emphasis back on to how we are living our life and creates a sense of urgency and a purpose. If we were to live for eternity, there would be no compulsion to strive to get things done. The 'deadline' of our mortality brings our life back into perspective. It provides the frame within which we have to work. Yalom expressed a similar sentiment when he said, 'Although the physicality of death destroys man, the idea of death saves him' (Yalom, 1980: 30). It takes the 'courage to be', as Tillich (1952) stated, to try to make sense of our lives, in spite of the fact that we are initially nothingness and must create and re-create ourselves and our lives in the face of death. Camus (1942) went even further when he argued that it was not just despite the fact of absurdity that we find meaning, but because of it. Only when we accept meaninglessness, do we become capable of perceiving or creating meaning.

Sartre: the original project

A sense of purpose is also created because we are orientated towards the future. Sartre (1943) believed that as nothingness we are always directed towards the future. We have to project ourselves into the future in order to create ourselves. This echoed Heidegger's description of human beings as thrown into the world, in time, moving always onwards towards a future and our inevitable end. The way in which we do project ourselves (or literally throw ourselves forward) is through what Sartre terms the 'original project'. He believed we have an ideal sense of ourselves, a direction we want to follow, a plan that we have committed ourselves to, even though we may not be aware of this. Our original project influences the choices we make and ultimately gives our life purpose. Although we may never accomplish our project by becoming this ideal self or even approximate it, as we may get side-tracked from our original project from time to time, the original project nevertheless gives us directionality and a path to follow in life.

Frankl: man's search for meaning

Purpose and meaning are the ways in which we make sense of our lives. Many of us may ponder the question 'what is the meaning of life?', which suggests a universal meaning, shared by all of us. However, Frankl – who is best known for his work on meaning and the absence of it when we are in dire circumstances – focused that question more sharply in order to ask: 'what is the meaning of *my* life?' He felt we needed to look for the answer within ourselves rather than seeking some universal truth. Sartre, too, stated that life has no meaning in general and that it is up to us as human beings to give it meaning. Heidegger (1927) linked meaning to understanding and stated that human beings could only determine what is meaningful or meaningless. Frankl believed that man's primary motivation was to find meaning: we are meaning creating beings. Frankl's work was based on his experiences in a concentration camp during World War II, which he later wrote about in his book *Man's Search for Meaning* (1946). What Frankl noticed during that time was that those who were able to find some meaning or purpose to their suffering, often holding on to ideas of what they would do after the war, were better able to survive the horrors of the camp. Frankl drew on Nietzsche's idea that: 'He who has a *why* to live for can bear almost any *how*' (Frankl, 1946: 126) as a way of understanding this phenomenon. This does not mean that finding meaning in a traumatic experience means finding the positive in the experience. Rather it is about how we make sense of that experience – how we are able to come to terms with what has happened to us and how that might change our perspective on how we live our lives. Frankl spoke of three ways of finding meaning. The first is by finding value in the things that we can take from the world, when we enjoy the good things in life. The second is by finding value by contributing something to the world, in a creative manner. The third is by finding value in our attitude towards inevitable suffering. This is very similar to Tillich's 'courage to be', which is always a courage we find in the face of challenge.

Meaning and purpose are inextricably linked, and give our lives both direction and substance, which help us to make sense of the experiences that we have. Meaning is the intrinsic sense we have of being connected to a web of things that matter, whereas purpose is the sense of direction we have towards creating greater meaning and achieving something that matters, often not just to ourselves but to others as well. A deep sense of meaning and purpose will help us make choices for ourselves in the present and for the future. It is not about looking for the positives in our experiences but more about looking at how things are connected and fit together. We discover what matters to us most and base our choices on that. In this way, we will live more deeply as we continue on a path that is most in tune with how we want to live. Quite often we discover that we have to seek out greater challenges and take on more problems before we begin to get that sense of how things fit together and where we fit into the picture. As we take on these challenges successfully, we get a greater sense of reality and validity. Frankl's interventions with his clients are often of this nature: challenging them to reinterpret their difficulties as an invitation to become braver and more able to face life.

14

Values and human worth

Our lives are value laden. Values are everywhere. Sartre spoke about values springing up like partridges all around us. Values tell us what we value, what is important, what has worth or how useful something is to us. Values create the texture of our lives. They are the lenses through which we interpret and understand the world. Values help us to make judgements and decisions about things around us and other people that we encounter in the world. They colour our lives and affect how we create meaning and purpose. Although other schools of therapy also see values and beliefs as important areas of exploration, the existential approach places particular emphasis on helping clients to discover what their values are and how these values are connected to the way they live and act in the world (Deurzen, 2012).

A philosophical examination of value

Both Heidegger (1927) and Sartre (1943) describe value as something that we, as individuals, place on an object, person, event or idea. What is valuable to one person may not be so to another. These philosophers argued that objects do not have any intrinsic value of their own, only the value we place on them. Sartre goes further and believes that value and being are interconnected: 'now we can ascertain more exactly what is the being of self: it is value' (Sartre, 1943: 92). What Sartre means by this is that, as part of the process of being, we give value. As soon as we reflect on something, we give it a value. This process of value giving is at the very core of being. What we value defines us and creates our very selfhood. This is linked to Heidegger's notion of 'care'. Because we are orientated towards the world as care, the world matters to us and through our connections to the world we make decisions about the way in which the things that we encounter matter by giving them value. Sartre reiterates this idea when he states that 'value is everywhere and nowhere' (ibid.: 95). Values disclose what we desire but also what we lack. Sartre believed that we would always make choices that were good for ourselves, even if those choices were not good for everyone. He believed that our choices confirm our values as we would always make good choices rather than bad ones.

Creating a personal value system

If objects and people do not possess intrinsic value, as the existential authors have suggested, then it is up to us to assign value ourselves. Our values arise out of what we feel we lack and what we desire. But they are also linked to our belief system. Our beliefs are also personal to us and are connected to our knowledge and understanding of the world. It is through our values and beliefs that we create a system of values and meanings to help us navigate life. This gives us a structure and direction to aim for, as values give us a personal understanding of what we are experiencing and guide us in our choices and responses to life. Deurzen and Adams state that values 'give us a feeling of integrity and connectivity' (Deurzen and Adams, 2011: 76), a way in which we can connect to the world in a personal way. However, as our value judgements are intrinsically connected to our way of being, we are often not explicitly aware of how we evaluate the world and what we are basing our beliefs on. Much of the time we take our values for granted and we avoid those things and people we don't value, acting as if they don't exist and don't matter. Our value system sometimes takes on a sense of permanence, values are just accepted, and beliefs are not questioned, they become sedimented (Strasser and Strasser, 1997). This idea of sedimentation came from Husserl and Merleau-Ponty, who showed that meanings get deposited, as debris gets deposited in the river and eventually blocks the flow of the river. Sartre went even further with this and spoke about mineralisation, where our meanings become gradually hardened, losing their very fluidity.

Hardening our meanings and setting them in stone gives us a sense of security and a sense of who we are, a framework for how we can live and respond to the world. It also gives us a sense of being more substantial, a way of guarding against the anxiety of not being a solid self. It is therefore a form of bad faith. By hardening our values and beliefs we pretend that we can be sure about ourselves and the world, when in reality nothing is certain. The positive side of this is that, as we are able to impose a value on something, we are also able to alter our values and beliefs. We sometimes hold on to values and beliefs that are no longer relevant in our lives and have become outdated. A gap emerges between what we believe in and our actual experience of the world or of ourselves. Many people underestimate their own capacity for change.

Human worth

If we are able to evaluate things that are external to ourselves, then we are also able to evaluate ourselves and our own human worth. Our sense of value is very much connected to our sense of self-esteem. We might have an idea of what we are good at, or what attributes we might possess, and these ideas develop out of our interactions with the world and with other people. However, there are also times when we might evaluate ourselves negatively, based on comments made by other people or how we have understood or made sense of certain experiences. These evaluations do not need to be static. They tend to change when what we find worthwhile in ourselves changes too. The existential approach focuses on this aspect of people's flexibility and capacity for making new choices and becoming more deliberate in the way they make decisions about themselves and their existence. We need to consider first what our values are, what they are based on and whether they are still relevant for our stage in life. We may also find that they are in contradiction with each other or are illogical. Letting go of long-held values and beliefs can give a person a great sense of release and can allow for a new perspective and new way of living to emerge.

15

A well-lived life

It is the question that most of us will contemplate more than any other in our lives: how can we live our life well? How do we live a good life? Some may consider that a good life involves having a good job or career, with a decent wage, or living with a certain level of comfort, and going on their favourite type of holidays. For others a good life involves living up to our principles, standing up for what we believe in and living in accordance with our values. Others still may see a good life as being about seeking pleasurable experiences and having artistic enjoyment, whereas there may be some people who feel it is about loving people and doing good things for others. Of course, for most of us, the idea of a good life will include many of these elements. There is no one right answer to this question, as there is no one right way of living our lives.

The question of living the good life has intrigued philosophers too, since the time of the Ancient Greeks and indeed in the East as well as in the West. Philosophers have been divided as to whether a good life is one that is pleasurable and happy, or whether the goodness of the person determines whether or not we have a good life. Socrates believed that we should be master of ourselves but also contribute to the community in which we live. He stated that 'it is not living, but living well which we ought to consider most important' (Plato, 1966: 48). For Socrates living well meant living according to our principles and values, living a life in tune with what we believe in.

Plato and Aristotle took their cue from Socrates and elaborated the distinction between a hedonistic, or pleasure based, lifestyle and a eudemonic, or value based, lifestyle. They showed the way towards a more thoughtful way of life where we can make those distinctions. They both clearly favoured a moral and reflective life over a pleasurable and comfortable life. Plato was famous for saying that the unreflective life is not worth living. Aristotle described many aspects of the world carefully, in order to enable people to live with more awareness and more ethically. He took the view that contributing something of value to the world around us is paramount.

Many later philosophers tried to find a way to combine these two modalities, of pleasurable and ethical living, in order to overcome the opposition. This often involved some form of control over our emotions. Epicurean living and stoical living are good examples of this.

For Epicurus (Konstan, 2016) a good life is a pleasurable one. He believed that we would always choose good over bad (or evil) and therefore we make good choices which enhance our pleasure and avoid bad choices which will lead to pain and suffering. He warned, however, that there also needs to be a balance and that having too much pleasure, i.e. overindulgence, should be avoided as it will ultimately lead to suffering. This is why an Epicurean way of life is a life where pleasure is sharply measured and carefully controlled in order to have just enough to feel able to enjoy and not so much that we become harmed by self-indulgence.

The Stoics took a different approach, which was to teach people how to overcome any hardship and difficulty by making themselves stronger and more able to endure suffering. If we become more resilient, then we do not have to be quite so careful and cautious and we can trust that we will be all right no matter what happens to us.

Later philosophers, such as Kant (1922) for instance, believed that leading a good life meant that one had to lead a morally good and upright life. He described what that entailed with great care and much detail. It was only in the nineteenth century that existential ideas about freedom and existential Angst came to the fore and led to a very different kind of exploration.

As we have already seen, Kierkegaard was the first truly existential philosopher. Although Kierkegaard (1843b) did not explicitly propose a theory of how to live well, he looked at the ways in which we can live and proposed a staged, developmental model of living. He noted that some people live in a hedonistic way, which he called the aesthetic stage. This involves living for ourselves, seeking pleasurable experiences and being generally comfort seeking.

Kierkegaard also noted that some people live with more awareness of themselves as part of a group. He called this the ethical stage, where we live in a moral way and make right or good choices which are determined by moral or religious values. However, for Kierkegaard these are both one dimensional ways of living (Mullen, 1995). People who live in these ways are lacking in passion and in personal commitment. They are not truly 'individual'. The third stage, the spiritual stage, is one where we take a leap of faith towards a more transcendental way of being. However, Kierkegaard's leap of faith can also be seen as a leap in temporality, where we move out of living within the constraints of the past, present and future and leap towards living towards eternity (see Figure 5.1). For Kierkegaard this was about creating a personal relationship between ourselves and God. A well-lived life would involve a spiritual union with God, where we would live in a loving fashion, challenging ourselves to be responsible to this higher authority for everything we did. It would not be about following the prescriptions of a priest or the Bible, but about thinking for ourselves. This is why Kierkegaard was considered to lack in Christianity.

Nietzsche (1882) went much further. He proclaimed that 'God is dead' and that we can no longer turn to any outside authority to find our answers about how to live. If there is no spiritual guide in our life, we are forced back on ourselves. A life lived well for Nietzsche would be one where we accept the tension between our animal instincts and our spiritual aspirations. Nietzsche believed that the objective of human existence was to overcome ourselves and develop our inner capacity for surpassing who we are, until we become an Übermensch, a superior human being. Nietzsche's idea of the eternal recurrence, which is that things will keep happening again and again, urges us to live each moment in the best possible way as if we had to repeat it for all eternity. There was a strong call on people to lift themselves above their lowly existence and show courage and determination to make something special of themselves.

An existential view of a well-lived life

Although there is no blueprint for living (Deurzen, 1988), there are certain assumptions contained within existential philosophy about what is important in how we should live and therefore what to consider if we are to create a well-lived life. The first is that we learn to think deeply about ourselves and the way we live. This is rather like what Socrates spoke about: to live reflectively. Thinking deeply about our lives means becoming more aware of our existence in all its reality: facing death, anxiety and guilt and understanding what these difficult experiences can tell us about what is important to us. Finding out what really matters to us helps us to understand what we value and believe. It is through facing up to the reality of our existence that we become stronger and wiser and can start to make more active and deliberate choices – choices based on what is important to us and what we value. Although this won't necessarily lead to happiness, we are more likely to live a more contented life if we live in accordance with our values and seek to make sense of and understand the experiences we have. We are also likely to embrace a range of other values, such as loving others, being kind, being strong, being truthful, being gentle and friendly, being just, being loyal and reliable, and many other such things.

Aristotle's view of a good life is particularly relevant here. When he speaks about aiming for 'eudaimonia', which some people, according to Macaro (2005), have misunderstood to mean happiness, he actually means living in tune with our values. Literally it means being in good connection with the spirit. Aristotle (1976) felt we should aim to live the best possible version of our life that we can enact or create for ourselves. He felt we should flourish at what we do but should also be virtuous and moral.

A well-lived life then requires a certain way of thinking. It involves deep reflection on how we live and awareness of the choices we make. It also means living so that we are true to ourselves and our values, but not at the expense of others. Essentially it requires us to live with a capacity for sustaining tension and conflict and paradox and in doing so find a certain flexibility, ease and balance.

Part 2

PRACTICAL FEATURES

16

Developing a phenomenological attitude

Part 1 of this book has shown how existential philosophy can provide us with insights into our existence and way of living. We have seen how philosophy can help us think about the various aspects of human existence that we all share. Existential therapy is a way of directly applying these insights to people's difficulties in living their lives. Understanding the existential issues that all of us contend with is the first step in doing so. Using a specific method in approaching human experience is the next step in the process. The existential approach to therapy therefore aims to help clients understand their own lives in a better, more direct and more reflective way. Drawing on philosophies of existence, existential therapists help clients to think deeply about their lives and question their assumptions, values and beliefs, which they often take for granted or are unaware of.

The existential approach to therapy is unique in its philosophical stance in relation to mental health. It takes the view that people are struggling with 'problems in living' (Szasz, 1961) and, rather than trying to diagnose and classify clients' problems, the existential approach aims to provide a pragmatic way of helping people to learn to help themselves. This means that clients will start working out how they can live in a better way from their own point of view and perspective.

The approach is truly a philosophical one as the philosophies of existence provide the theoretical grounding. But existential therapy also uses applied philosophical methods such as dialectics, hermeneutics, maieutics and perhaps most importantly phenomenology. We shall talk about some of these other methods later, but we shall start by giving a brief précis of phenomenology. Phenomenology is a way of grasping the whole of reality from many different angles and perspectives. It seeks to combine objectivity and subjectivity and it requires us to be systematic in the way we consider things. This fosters a certain attitude in how existential therapists approach their clinical work and the world in general. The phenomenological attitude begins by developing a sense of wonderment about the world, a questioning stance from which to approach not only the client's but also the therapist's own position in the world.

Edmund Husserl

Phenomenology, the science of phenomena, was developed by Edmund Husserl, as we discussed above. He aimed to found a new, more human and complex form of science, to give us a way of studying the human experience of things in the world. Husserl was particularly influenced by Brentano's concept of intentionality (Chapter 6) and wanted to get back to 'the things themselves', to seek to explore the phenomena of experience in a fresh way. Husserl felt that as part of everyday living our experiences were clouded by layers of interpretation and presumption. Whilst it is crucial for our survival to be able to recognise certain experiences and respond quickly based on our analysis and understanding, in doing so we lose the uniqueness of the experience and something of its quality. In this way, our responses tend to be based on our assumptions and hypotheses about things rather than on a thorough understanding of what is happening. Husserl believed that through connecting to our experiences more directly we are able to determine the meaning of what we are experiencing. This allows us to come to know the world in a more real, more intimate and more complex way.

Phenomenological investigation

Husserl developed a way of investigating the phenomena of experience by performing a number of reductions. In the first instance phenomenology asks us to step away from our natural attitude of making judgements about our world. We do this by suspending our belief in our own capacity for knowing things straight away. We then bracket our previous assumptions about the world and take a step back to observe the things themselves, as they actually are, anew. This particular 'reduction' is often referred to as the phenomenological reduction. The first step here is to bracket (or suspend, which is called the epoché) all presuppositions so that the focus remains on the phenomenon rather than on how we make sense of the phenomenon, as we have often done before. Epoché requires us to be open and to focus our attention on our consciousness, so that we are aware of the knowledge we hold about the world, including our beliefs and values and the assumptions and bias that we carry. The bracketing does not mean trying to get rid of our assumptions and be value free, but rather to set these aside momentarily in order to be able to understand and be aware of what those assumptions are. We can thus revisit our experience from a different perspective and also become aware of our own bias. Epoché is about being open and trying to see things anew as if we were experiencing them for the first time. When we are in a new situation or meet someone from a culture or place we haven't yet experienced, we tend to ask more questions. The more familiar an experience or situation is, the fewer questions we ask, as we draw on what we already know and the opinions we have already formed. So, we try to be fresh in our approach, and we do this by setting what we observe against the perspective of its own horizon. We equalise our attention and try to spread our attention evenly around all aspects of what we are experiencing, rather than jumping to conclusions.

The second step involves what Husserl terms the eidetic reduction. This refers to the word 'eidos', or 'shape', which means that we are now going to focus on the object of our awareness rather than on the process of our awareness, as we did earlier. The purpose of this second reduction is to try to grasp the essence of the phenomenon in front of us, to penetrate through to its actual presentation, in trying to attain its 'universal and unchangeable structures' (Husserl, 1985: 636). We bear in mind that things are never stagnant but show themselves to us in many different guises and from many angles. We both register the variety and dynamic movement of what we observe and also try to grasp the essential aspects of it that remain the same.

By varying how we think about an object or situation we can discover what remains constant, and this then is its essence. It helps to examine the object of our attention from different angles and at different times. It may also be helpful to get views from elsewhere. We try to go around the houses to examine the phenomenon in question as thoroughly as we can.

The final step is the transcendental reduction where we aim to go beyond the specific observation of this particular thing through describing the essence of the phenomenon in order to see the world and our interactions with it in a new way, with new meanings; 'the world ceases to be a self-evident given and becomes instead a gift of meaning' (Kearney, 1994: 20). In the transcendental reduction I aim to become aware of my own experience as a subject of the experience, in order to stop being personal about it and transcend my own subjective take on it towards an intersubjective, connective understanding. This is when we become aware of the way in which our experiences are connected to those of others and we can relativise our own perspective. We see our own point of view as relative and yet as connected to the points of view of all other people.

The phenomenological attitude of the existential therapist therefore involves becoming aware of how we think about and see the world and how the impact of our particular view of the world will influence what we experience. Putting our assumptions aside we can attempt to see the world, especially the world of the client, anew, becoming inquisitive and questioning and helping our clients to do the same. Through describing and questioning themselves, clients can grasp what remains constant (the essence) and where there is flexibility in their worldview and in their experience. Clients are then encouraged to reflect on these observations and uncover new meanings and new understandings of themselves and their world, expanding their awareness and, with it, their possibilities. Meanwhile as therapists we are immersed in their experience and find a way of seeing what about it is universal and shared, on the one hand, and specific and personal, on the other hand. We aim to become truly intersubjective with our clients, recognising that their understanding of their world will change our understanding of our own world as well.

17

The quality of the therapeutic relationship

I-Thou

The success of any approach to psychotherapy is largely dependent on the quality of the therapeutic relationship between the therapist and client (Norcross, 2002). In this respect, the existential approach is no different. For the client to be able to talk openly about their life and to be able to question it and reflect deeply on their way of living, they need to be able to develop a trusting and close relationship with their therapist.

The existential therapeutic relationship shares many similarities with other approaches. It is a person-centred approach in that the focus of the sessions is on the client's preoccupations and concerns and on how they understand these and make sense of their lives in general. The existential therapist is open to working with whatever clients bring and will focus on any issues that are most pressing to them. Exploration of any issue will usually highlight the specific way in which each person experiences their existence and way of living. It will show where the client is having difficulties and it will also bring to light what is missing and what is not being said. In every statement and every communication, the blocks that a person may be struggling with will be evident. Their values and beliefs will be hidden close to the surface. Therefore, each exploration will also focus on the assumptions clients hold about themselves, other people and the world in general. Therefore, the existential therapist needs to be open in their attitude, as described in the previous chapter. By taking an inquisitive and explorative attitude to the client and the client's life, the therapist engages deeply with the person's world and instils a new sense of awe in the client for all there is to know about them. Now clients will begin to become inquisitive about themselves as well. This is also a way in which the therapist can demonstrate their 'care', from a Heideggerian perspective. The therapist, with this intimate focus, indicates that the client matters and that their difficulties in living are well worth grappling with.

Probably the most distinctive aspect of the existential therapeutic relationship is that it is a 'real' relationship (Cohn, 1997). A 'real' therapeutic relationship is one where the therapist is a co-traveller on the journey of exploration, rather than someone in a position of power, where knowledge is handed down to the client. The existential therapist is humble, seeing the client as an expert in themselves with the therapist as a mentor who helps them search for and find their own truth. Deurzen (2012) suggests that living is an art and that, as with any art, it takes practice and refinement. The existential practitioner therefore allows knowledge and wisdom to emerge from the joint exploration. This is also demonstrated in the way that the client and therapist communicate in the session. It becomes more of a dialogue and discussion than a monologue which is then analysed and interpreted. When there is a true exchange and a real encounter, the relationship deepens.

Martin Buber: **I-Thou**

Humility, inquisitiveness and openness all point to a certain quality of the therapeutic relationship. Martin Buber, a philosopher and theologian, was interested in the way in which we relate to each other. He determined that there are two ways of relating, which he termed *I-Thou* and *I-It* (Buber, 1929). Buber noted that one of the ways in which people related to each other, and the world, was as if the other was an object – something to be used or experienced. When we relate to a person in this way, in an *I-It* way, we are not listening to the other to understand them; instead we may be thinking about how we can catalogue or judge or analyse the person. We may be getting preoccupied too much with how we are being affected by what they are saying, or what we might want to say next, rather than trying to really understand the other from their own standpoint. *I-Thou*, in contrast, is a meeting of two people, where each tries to understand the other, not in an objective way but by gaining a full picture and a subjective understanding, to feel what it would be like to stand and walk in the other's shoes. In these *I-Thou* moments, we do not experience the other as a person separate from us; we are fully immersed in the moment of meeting and relating and engaged in connecting with the other in a deep way. As soon as we reflect on this meeting or on the other, we move out of the *I-Thou* and back into an *I-It* mode of relating. Buber was interested in how we meet each other in our relations; *I-Thou* is a combining, holistic way of relating and *I-It* is a separating mode of relating. In the *I-Thou* mode I see the whole of the person instead of only a part. In the *I-Thou* mode I see the person's possibilities unfold in front of them, instead of seeing only their past. Buber also understood that the way in which I relate to the other is the way I relate to myself too. I become an object to myself when I make the other an object and I come into my own possibilities when I see the other's potential too.

Therefore, in the therapy session the existential therapist will endeavour to create moments of *I-Thou*, where the therapist will attempt to meet the client, focusing all their attention on trying to understand the client and their difficulties. In those moments, the client in turn will feel truly listened to and understood and therefore able to listen and understand themselves as well. It is this quality of the therapeutic relationship that is so important – the meeting of two people and the creation of something new happening between them in the session. We know this is happening when silence in the room feels comfortable, deep and thoughtful rather than tense or frightening.

18

A descriptive exploration

Description, rather than explanation (Deurzen and Adams, 2016; Spinelli, 2002), is the defining feature of existential therapy. When we start to explain something, two things happen. The first is that further dialogue and exploration are closed down as we get the feeling that our experience, under discussion, becomes solidified, almost like an object: to be examined. The second is that an explanation prompts the need for a cause. It presents the experience as if it is linear and can be viewed in terms of cause and effect. It is sometimes difficult not to fall into this as our social world is often construed in this linear manner. When we visit our GP to discuss a particular symptom, for example, we are looking for a simple explanation and indeed for the cause of how we are feeling. But physical health is very different from mental and emotional health, which cannot so easily be reduced to a simple cause and effect experience. The way we feel fluctuates and is composed of many different aspects of experience at many different levels. We feel the way we feel because of multiple and complex reasons. Yet clients may still ask, 'Why am I feeling like this?' or 'What makes me do the things I do?', to which the therapist may be tempted to offer a simple explanation about why the client may be feeling in a certain way. But when we do so, we lose something of the richness of the lived experience. We also assume that an experience or feeling can be explained away when it actually has to be engaged with. Allowing clients to describe their experience as fully as possible, not to seek an explanation but to understand the experience better, will enable them to see their experience differently, and from a different perspective. Out of this exploration, understanding and meaning can be found, especially when they begin to realise that their experience is fluid and dynamic and constantly changes. They learn to explore and examine instead of classifying their experience.

Staying at the level of description is essential if existential therapists are to work in a phenomenological way, without pre-judging the situation and without fitting clients into a theoretical or diagnostic framework. However, it does require a different and more engaged way of listening. It has become habitual for therapists to be trained to listen attentively to the client whilst at the same time working out what symptoms are being presented and how these can be categorised. Therapists are encouraged to work out how to frame the clients' words within their own theoretical framework in order to analyse and interpret the meaning of what the client is saying. Existential therapists listen differently. They listen to understand the client and their struggles and connect to and make sense of the client's own framework of meaning. The therapist is listening to understand how the client lives in the world, what their relationships are like, how they think about themselves and their predicaments and what their values and beliefs are. Open questions are asked of the client to gain clarity, and the existential therapist adopts a naïve stance towards the client, questioning and exploring rather than assuming. Keeping to the level of description, the client's world is opened up and thus we are able to access richer, more detailed accounts and probe more deeply into the client's experience. By using *how* and *what* questions, the therapist seeks to help the client to describe what their experience is and how they feel about it. In this way therapist and client search together for the way in which the client makes meaning. This is what is meant by a hermeneutic approach: to interpret meanings as they are actually experienced from the inside instead of by attributing meaning from the outside.

Challenging bias

In order to do this exploration of meaning we have to accept that everyone of us is biased, because bias is the leading edge of our interpretation of the world. We see the world through a particular lens and colour our experiences accordingly. We can begin to become aware of this bias by examining our underlying assumptions about the world.

This is something that applies as much to the client as to the therapist. Each has their own bias and assumptions and we need to find a way of filtering and clarifying these. It is all too easy to think we know what someone is talking about, especially if that person is talking about something we have experienced. The task of the existential therapist is to be aware of how we are making assumptions. When the client says that they are feeling depressed, we might have an idea of what depression is or how the client might be feeling, such as having a low mood or lacking motivation or feeling despair or self-loathing, but we don't know exactly how depression feels to that particular person. Asking the client to describe their experience enables both the client and the therapist to understand their unique struggles and forces us to begin to pay proper attention to what life is actually like for the client.

Challenging assumptions is not only focused on the client's experiences but also on the words that they use. Our shared language, crucial for communication, is another area in which we can make wrong assumptions. The meaning behind one person's use of a word can be quite different from another's. The existential therapist will check out what clients mean when they say certain words. They do not take for granted that they know what the client means. The focus is therefore on questioning, searching, exploring, clarifying and understanding.

Equalisation and horizontalisation

As part of the descriptive exploration, existential therapists keep an open mind as to what is important to the client. Client's often talk about several difficulties in a session or describe many facets of one issue. The aim of equalisation is to keep all aspects in mind and open to exploration. Therefore, it is important not to create a hierarchy too soon and not to decide on what the client should focus on, but instead to allow the things of importance to emerge by themselves and let the client shape the landscape.

In doing so we also bear in mind that there is a constant shifting of space and time and we keep an eye on the horizon of the client's experience. We remain sensitive to the way in which experiences are formed and impacted on by the limits of the client's horizon. The familial, social, political and cultural pressures on the person are not immediately obvious or in sight, but we bear in mind that they exist at the edge of the person's awareness. These things determine the person's experience and perspective and the more we explore a person's position in the world and see what surrounds them, the better we can encompass the whole of their life. An emphasis on description, challenging assumptions and keeping an open mind on what is important to the client are the keystones to this process. However, the descriptive aspect is just one element of the way in which existential therapists work and it is often used extensively at the beginning stages of the therapeutic process.

19

Taking stock and being aware of the limitations of life

Change

Most clients come to therapy because they are dissatisfied and want to change some aspect of their lives. The existential approach is different from other approaches in that it does not make change an explicit goal of the therapy. Change is the bedrock of life, from an existential perspective. It is not something we need to bring about. We rather need to take awareness of how we are stopping natural and organic, constant change by trying to remain the same. Change is not something we need to strive towards. Rather, change is often an inevitable outcome of the process of thinking deeply about our lives and questioning the way in which we are living. The focus of existential therapy therefore remains firmly on the open exploration of the client's life. For some clients, what changes is their attitude or perspective on their life, and this in turn will bring about fundamental changes to the way they live and interact with the world. By understanding ourselves better, we are better able to take ownership of our choices, which may include actively choosing to continue with a similar way of living or gradually releasing our desire and capacity for going for new ways of life by becoming more conscious of the range of options and striking out on unknown paths.

Taking stock

Before any changes can be made to ourselves or to our lives, or before we can find solutions to the problems we experience, we need to have an understanding of what our life is currently like, in all its diversity and complexity. We need to get a sense of how we relate to ourselves and others and where our difficulties lie. Other therapeutic approaches may home in on the issues that bring the client to therapy, helping them to find strategies to overcome these issues or challenges. Whilst existential therapists will also focus on the importance of these presenting issues, the existential approach does this through taking a more holistic approach. The emphasis is on gaining an understanding of the person as a whole: how they interact with others, how they connect to the world and how they view themselves and their purpose, values and objectives. These will all influence and play a part in their experience of the world, but it is likely that they have never reflected on them.

Deurzen (2012) posits the need to take stock of our lives, and the initial phase of existential therapy focuses on this self-reflective task. Clients are helped to understand themselves and how their world is lived, organised and constructed, in ever-greater depth. Deurzen describes three aspects of taking stock. The first is to recognise the assumptions we make about the world, on all four dimensions of existence (see Chapter 20). As we saw in the previous chapter, these assumptions need to be clarified but also questioned. By understanding the basis of our assumptions, we can begin to check them against our experience but also to examine what they say about our values and the beliefs we have about the world in general.

The second aspect involves tuning in to the values that we hold. Values can help us to understand what we like and what is important to us. However, we are not always aware of what our values are and how they influence the decisions we make or how different values might be at odds with each other. Our values are often embedded in the things we say and need to be recognised and made explicit, so that we can determine what guides our choices and decisions. Defining values is an important aspect of existential therapy, as it is through identifying our values and beliefs that we are able to create more meaningful lives.

The final aspect of taking stock involves highlighting our personal talents. Finding out what we are good at and what we enjoy will help us gain an understanding of what is possible to achieve. Helping a person to build on their talents, skills and passions enables them to feel confident and comfortable in trying something new. However, we also need to be aware of our limitations, both our personal limitations and those imposed upon our existence. It is important to have a realistic understanding of what our potential is and how we might address the possibilities and challenges presented to us by life.

Limit situations

Freedom and free will are important aspects of existential philosophy and one of the strengths of this way of looking at the world is to hold in awareness the paradox that freedom is only possible because of limits and within limitations. Jaspers (1951) highlighted how there are certain situations that we face in life that are unavoidable. We cannot change these situations, we can only acknowledge and learn how best to respond to them. Jaspers called these situations limit situations. He said: 'I must die, I must suffer, I must struggle, I am subject to chance, I involve myself inexorably in guilt' (Jaspers, 1951: 20). Taking stock, therefore, involves understanding not only our present existence but also what is truly possible or impossible in the future. Clients will seek to uncover their personal talents and abilities, but reflect upon them realistically, by looking at their personal limitations as well as their potential. Speaking openly about the limitations that the world holds for us in terms of the limit situations that we all have to face, in the society we are part of, the body we inhabit and the physical environment we live in as well as in terms of the person we are, often brings greater clarity and with that greater courage to reengage with life in a more real way.

20

Getting the bigger picture

Four dimensions of existence

Existential philosophy has demonstrated the interconnected nature of human beings. We are not isolated beings or self-contained entities, instead we connect to the world and with others in myriad different ways and our web of connections expands far and wide. However, if we only look at individuals from one perspective or one point of view, then we get a much-reduced view of that person. Binswanger (1946) and Boss (1979), the first practitioners to apply existential ideas to psychiatry, recognised this limitation. Binswanger, in particular, saw the restrictive nature of the medical model, where individuals were reduced to their pathology and the sum of their symptoms. The therapeutic work was aimed at classifying and devising treatment plans to reduce or eliminate symptoms. Binswanger, however, felt that if the focus was primarily on the clients' behaviour, then only one aspect of the individual was being acknowledged. He felt that clients brought their whole world into the therapy room, not just their presenting issues or difficulties and not just their behaviours, but the entirety of their experience as human beings. Therefore, in order to be able to help those clients effectively, the clients' symptoms would need to be included in a more holistic approach, which took into account the person's whole universe. How clients cope with the life experiences that they have had, or the difficulties they have suffered, will be influenced by their social relationships and how much support they have, their view about themselves as individuals and their hopes and aspirations for what they feel is possible in their future. The client's world is important as it is the ground from which they understand their predicaments and defines the range of possible solutions they can draw on. Binswanger recognised this aspect of human existence and sought to find a systematic way in which a client's world can be investigated. Through this process the therapist and client would both gain a new perspective on the client's difficulties and challenges.

Binswanger's worldview

Binswanger was inspired by Heidegger's (1927) concept of *being-in-the-world*. He agreed with the idea that as human beings we are always in relation to the situation in which we find ourselves, be that with other people, our physical environment or ourselves. Binswanger was particularly interested in Heidegger's concept of *being-with* (*Mitsein*) and wanted to find a way of incorporating this into his clinical work with his patients. He also drew on the work of von Uexküll (1921) who had posited a biological world-concept through his observations of animal relationships. Von Uexküll observed that animals related to their environment or *Umwelt* in two ways, through the world of perception (*Merkwelt*) and through a world of action (*Aktionwelt*). These world-concepts elucidated by von Uexküll allowed Binswanger to formulate a framework for human beings. He wanted to find a structure with which to investigate a person's world in greater depth. Binswanger noted that our relations with the world were not purely confined to how we respond to our physical environment but extend to the way in which we relate to others and to ourselves. He took a worldview approach to human beings to highlight the different ways in which we relate and the different ways there are of *being-in-the-world*. As Binswanger explains: 'This *materialité* of the world-design, originating from the 'key' (*Gestimmtheit*) of the existence, is by no means confined to the environment, to the world of things, or to the universe in general, but refers equally to the world of one's fellow men (*Mitwelt*) and to the self-world (*Eigenwelt*)' (Binswanger, 1946: 212).

Four dimensions of existence

In his book *The Discovery of Being* (1983) Rollo May further clarified and refined the worldviews that were proposed by Binswanger into three dimensions of existence: the *Umwelt,* the *Mitwelt* and the *Eigenwelt*. The *Umwelt*, similar to von Uexküll's conception, represented the physical environment of the person, or the 'world around'. However, this dimension also represents our body's biological world, as well as the world of objects and the environment we live in. The *Mitwelt*, in line with Binswanger's formulation, is the 'with world', the world of the other and our social relationships. Finally, the *Eigenwelt* is our 'own world' and is the dimension of the self and our relationship to ourselves (May, 1946: 126). A fourth dimension, the *Überwelt*, was added later in 1988 by Deurzen. This dimension represents our world of ideas and values, our spiritual world, where we relate to purpose and meaning, but also to what is beyond us and what moves us forward. The spiritual dimension of human existence could also be considered as the philosophical or the ideological aspect of what we are. It is very evident in the existential literature, especially in the work of authors such as Kierkegaard, Buber, Tillich and Marcel. This dimension has considerable impact on how we understand and make sense of our lives. The four dimensions are represented graphically in Figure 20.1.

Deurzen has developed Binswanger's and May's concept of the worldview further, formulating it into a framework for existential therapists to use in their practice. She has written about the four dimensions of existence extensively (1988, 2005 with Arnold-Baker, 2010, 2012, and 2016 with Adams), showing each dimension to be the playground of paradoxes and contradictions and demonstrating how therapists can use this framework of tensions on four dimensions to clarify the client's worldview. The framework is not limited to the function of formulation and clarification of a person's worldview, but rather it is a way of systematically exploring the client's world and examining the paradoxes and contradictions of existence that clients will come up against in their life on all four dimensions. Each of the four dimensions will be examined in greater detail over the next four chapters.

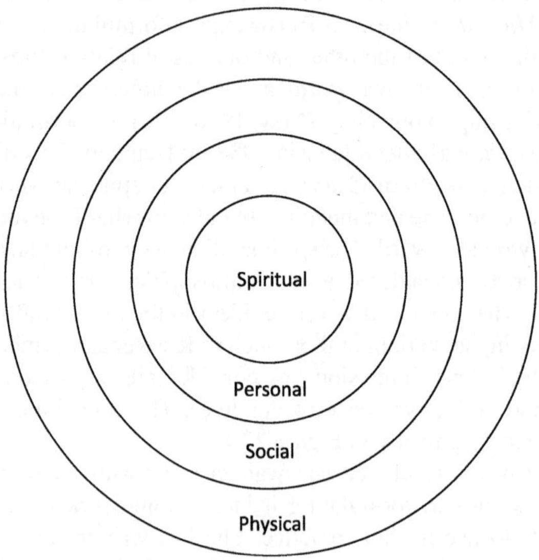

Figure 20.1 Four dimensions of existence

21

Living in the world physically

The physical dimension, or *Umwelt*, is the world into which we are *thrown*, as Heidegger would say. It is the natural world that existed before we were born and that will remain after we die. 'It is the world of natural law and natural cycles of sleep and awakeness, of being born and dying, desire and relief' (May, 1983: 126). It is the dimension of material things and the world of action. It concerns our relations to our physical environment through our body and concerns, where we live – whether in a city or in the countryside, beside the sea or in the mountains – and where we feel at home. The physical dimension also relates to the forces of nature we encounter, the weather, the elements – fire, air, water and earth – and how we connect to that natural environment. The physical dimension also contains the world of animals and birds, both wild and domestic, and our relationships with them. These physical elements of our environment are part of the givens of our existence; they involve aspects that we have no control over, such as natural disasters – hurricanes, earthquakes and volcanoes. Existential therapists will help their clients to explore how they respond to their environment and to the aspects over which they have no control. Does the client feel at the mercy of their environment or able to show mastery in being able to adapt and be flexible towards whatever life throws at them?

The counterpart to the environment, or rather the complement to it, is our own bodily existence. The body we were born with and our genetic make-up are also beyond our control and represent our thrownness. Although we are able to have an impact on our body through our diet, our engagement with the environment, our activity, training, practice and fitness, there are fundamental aspects of our own physical presence in the world that we have to accept cannot be changed. We will never have wings and won't be able to defy gravity.

We will never be immortal, no matter how much we would like to imagine that we can live forever. Our bodies are also of a particular kind and nature. We are born with a particular sex, male or female, and though we may defy this by adopting a different gender, our bodies will still remember their origin. The same is true for the size of our bodies; if we are born tall, we shall never be small. We may try to change our size but will have to work with the equipment we were given, and this brings us up against certain limits. How we respond and relate to our bodily experience will impact on our perceptions of our body image. This will affect how we feel about our body in general and whether we perceive ourselves as strong and vital or weak and vulnerable. Our thoughts about our body will define what we feel is possible for us to do in an embodied way. The existential therapist will help clients to explore how they present themselves bodily to the world, in terms of their confidence and their gestures, but also through their use of clothes and other forms of physical expression. Embodied existence is much more complex than people think. It involves our food preferences, our like or dislike for travel and for high or low temperatures, our reactions to illness or injury, our comfort with closeness and intimacy, our relationship to animals, the way we sit and drink our tea, wash our hands or clean our teeth. Our animal presence in the world is also about smell and texture and safety and exploration.

How aware we are of our bodily needs and how attuned we are to our senses are all part of our relationship to the physical dimension. This includes our relationship to food and drink, how we feed ourselves and how aware we are of our hunger or feelings of satiety. The amount and quality of sleep we have will also impact on our well-being and can be an area where clients experience difficulties, often as a result of their lack of trust in abandoning their bodies to a state of rest and relaxation. Sexuality and how we are as sexual beings are also connected to our bodily needs as well as how we experience ourselves in an embodied way. The physical dimension of our bodily being is therefore an area of exploration which will enable the client, and therapist, to gain a deeper understanding of the person, and how their understanding and awareness in the physical dimension will form part of their beliefs about themselves and the world in general.

As we said in the previous chapter, van Deurzen (2010 and 2012) noted that in each dimension there are tensions and paradoxes that we face. In the physical dimension the basic tension is between life and death, as it is into the physical dimension that we are born and will die. Existential therapists will explore how clients face the tensions and paradoxes that are contained within this dimension. Some of the predictable tensions created by the conflict between life and death are our constant pursuit of health in the face of potential illness, our desire for comfort and security contrasted with our fear of insecurity and discomfort, and our pursuit of wealth and ease in response to our dread and avoidance of destitution and poverty. The emphasis in this dimension is on the need for safety and survival. Clients may strive for one side of the polarity, say health, in the hope of denying the existence of its opposite, i.e. illness. But in actual fact life is a constant balancing act between wellness and unwellness and we have to learn to embrace both ends of the equation and not seek to avoid the polarity. If we face the negatives, we are more able to make the most of the positives. The objective is to be in balance and to become adaptable and flexible in the face of the natural and biological challenges that we inevitably have to face in this dimension. As May highlighted, our experience in the physical dimension is all about adaptation and adjustment: 'I adapt to the cold weather and I adjust to the periodic needs of my body for sleep' (May, 1983: 128). But before we can make those adjustments to our lives and perceptions, we need to be aware of and tuned into what our senses and body are telling us.

Clients who have difficulties in the physical dimension are most often people who are switched off from their organic experience. They may present with issues around eating disorders, addiction, compulsion, psychosomatic illnesses or phobias (Deurzen, 2010: 290). However, the exploration of such issues should never be limited to an exploration of the physical dimension, as there will be many repercussions on different levels as well. Similarly, we should never forget to ground each person's experience in their physical world.

Exploration of each dimension will highlight clients' strengths and weaknesses, the talents they hold and the challenges they face. The dimensions are utterly interwoven and interrelated. Mastery in one dimension may help clients face challenges in another dimension and thus allow for creative solutions to life's difficulties.

22

Living in the world socially

While our bodily existence is the most fundamental aspect of being human, the relationships we have with other people also form an important part of our lives. This is true even for those who try to isolate themselves, which is in itself a response to the presence of other people in the world. We cannot avoid being greatly affected by the existence of other people and deal with this issue on a daily basis. Looking at the physical dimension of life demonstrated how interconnected we are with our environment and the physical world around us. In the social dimension we are equally interconnected, but this time it is with the other people in our existence. The social dimension, therefore, is the world of our relationships with other people. It is the *with* world (*Mitwelt*), where we are in *being with others*. Heidegger (1927) noted that there is no avoiding the fact that we are always in relation to other people, and Sartre (1943) highlighted that it is through other people, and our relationships with them, that we get a sense of ourselves. Other people can see us in a way we cannot see ourselves and their feedback makes us self-aware. This is also why Sartre took the view that hell is other people, because other people have a tremendous amount of power over us. Our relationships with others affect not only our feelings and emotions and our very freedom of thought and movement, but also how we relate to and understand ourselves.

The social dimension to a large extent takes place in the public world and concerns the way in which we interact, but also how we portray ourselves to others and how we present ourselves in a public way. The social dimension includes all our relationships to other people. When we think of our relationships, those that come most easily to mind will be the ones we have with our family and friends. They are the people in our lives who are likely to be the most important to us and who will have the biggest impact on us, both positively and negatively. However, we also relate to other people in many ways, from study or work colleagues to people we know in passing, or people we come into contact with in our everyday living, our doctor, shop workers and postman, for example. We also relate to strangers that we pass on the street or stand next to in a queue. Furthermore, we relate to the anonymous crowd of all the people we know to be alive in the world.

In consequence our social world is not only confined to our daily social relationships, but it also includes our relationship to our culture and the society we live in. How much synergy or tension there exists between our own values and beliefs and the cultural and societal values of the country in which we live will determine how comfortable we feel or how at odds we might feel with everyone around us. Existential therapists will also help clients to explore how they relate to the cultural, social and political norms they are inserted within and the impact these might have on how they think and feel about themselves.

The language we use and how we communicate with others comprise another aspect of the social fabric of our world. Can we make ourselves understood? Can we understand what other people really mean? When miscommunication occurs, how does it happen and who does it happen with? All these areas are worth exploring in the social dimension. The existential therapist will encourage each client to explore the ways in which they relate or do not relate to others. Noting avoidance and becoming cognisant of where difficulties lie, and of how clients respond to conflict, are hugely important and engaging, but the work will also involve highlighting the good and nourishing relationships the client has created and how they are contributing to others in relationship.

The social dimension of life is about affiliation. Belonging and rejection form the main tension and paradox in the social dimension and as human beings we oscillate between these two poles of experience. The main question in this dimension is: where do I belong? How much am I giving myself over to others and how much am I holding back? How immersed am I in social relationships or how withdrawn am I? Do I feel accepted or rejected? Am I integrated or isolated? Do I feel affinity or repulsion? Am I merged or am I separated? We establish how the person is in the world with others and whether the client has lots of friendships or only one or a few special ones. The existential therapist will help the client explore how they relate with others and whether they are competitive or cooperative, submissive or dominant, engaged or withdrawn. The existential therapist will help map out the various ways in which the client relates, highlighting patterns or modes of relating. Understanding our social relationships is important as they are linked to our emotional well-being. We connect to other people in an emotional way and our relationships with others will often determine how we feel about ourselves. At the basis of all relationships is a need for mutual support and acknowledgement. However, love is the greater good we strive towards. Love is a stronger bond, where we allow the other to become so close that they are part of our inner world. Our intimate relationships are therefore not included in the social dimension as they move us into the personal dimension and connect to feelings about the self.

The majority of clients seeking therapy will bring relational issues of one kind or another. Difficulties on this dimension will include bullying, sibling rivalry, sadism and sociopathy or neediness, masochism, hypochondria or hysteria (Deurzen, 2010: 290). The aim of an existential exploration of the client's social dimension is to help them become more aware of how they relate to others and how they involve themselves in conflict and how they might find ways to compromise, negotiate or cooperate. Highlighting for the client how they can understand their emotional responses to social situations may guide them in creating better relationships for themselves based on better communication, closer bonds of trust and greater compassion for each other.

23

Living in the world personally

As we have seen, the way we relate to people in the social world can shift into that intimate dimension that is our personal world. In our inner world we are not so much outward facing as looking inwards. The personal dimension of existence concerns how we connect to ourselves in a very individual and intimate way. This represents our personal domain. In the physical and social dimensions, we are faced with the givens of existence; our locus of control is limited to how we respond to the external world of things and people. We aim for acceptance, flexibility and adaptation as we negotiate our interconnections with the world that we are part of. The personal dimension, however, is different, because at its centre there is a dynamic sense of selfhood, which we have the power to create and re-create.

The personal dimension is the world of the self and identity, where we feel a sense of authority and ownership. It is where we develop a sense of ourselves, by reflecting on the feedback received from our interactions with the external world. As we connect with other people, we gain a feel for who we are in their eyes and who we can never be. Similarly, in the physical dimension we discover what our bodies are good at doing and what they find difficult. This too we integrate into our reflection on what we can be as a person. We discover what personal characteristics we have, what traits we exhibit and what attitudes and opinions we hold. We come to recognise how we create a consistent and coherent sense of ourselves through our confirmation of these traits and characteristics. Some people have a strong sense of themselves, whereas others have a more fluid sense, and others again may feel it is difficult to define themselves at all. Some of our experiences may be contradictory and this might be confusing.

The personal dimension also concerns what is special about us as individuals. What are our talents and special qualities? What makes us unique and different? But also, what qualities do we share with others? How are we similar and normal and do we fit in with the world? How do we stand out? These questions of identity are all aspects which are explored intensely by existential therapists. But of course they are explored within the context of the existential understanding that there is no such thing as a solid or stable self. All of us are bodies that are in relationship with others. But we are also conscious and we reflect on our own existence, on our possibilities and our limitations. We are onto-dynamic, and always in movement.

The exploration of the personal dimension will include many aspects of a person's changing relationship to themselves. Their thoughts about themselves, about others and about the world at large will fluctuate a great deal and we remain open to that evolving picture of each person. Clients seeking therapy will often report difficulties on the personal dimension, citing that they wish to stop feeling unhappy about an aspect of themselves or their lives. The existential therapist will help clients to elucidate their thoughts and understanding so that they gain a deeper sense of what they are and how they connect to themselves and the world around them.

The personal dimension is about identity and our work at this level always involves a confrontation with a person's anxiety and despair about themselves. It will also open the productive tracing of existential doubt and guilt and of a person's sense of freedom, responsibility and choice. Areas of exploration will centre on the way the person experiences anxiety and how this experience influences the choices they make. How does this person embrace or deny their freedom to change? Do they experience guilt and if so what is it connected to? How has the person failed to live up to his or her potential? These are some of the areas of exploration that existential therapists will encourage their clients to engage with on this dimension.

Therapy will inevitably involve self-reflection and it is through this intimate scrutiny and self-challenge that clients gain an understanding of themselves in a deeper sense. In terms of the polarities on this dimension they are about strength and weakness, as well as about authenticity versus inauthenticity. This polarity concerns how we can find our way as an autonomous individual in a world that is full of other people. It is about how we hold our own and take possession of our world, on the one hand, and let go of our illusions of grandiosity, on the other hand. We will remember that Heidegger (1927) described the way in which authenticity and inauthenticity are both aspects of our everyday existence. He showed how these were intrinsically related to our capacity for facing up to our mortality and our limited strength or perfection. It is impossible for any human being to only make authentic choices. We do need to get on with living in the physical world and fall in with others and their ideas and ways of living some of the time. We are constantly finding a balance between perfecting ourselves and coming up against our own limitations as well.

We are able to cultivate a sense of strength concerning how we see ourselves and how confident or sure we are, but will invariably come up against the other side of ourselves as well. Our weakness and the recognition of our vulnerability and limited capability are also what makes us sensitive. As always, both sides of the equation have to be taken into account.

In terms of the difficulties on this dimension, those who have a strong sense of themselves may be boastful, egocentric in their views of themselves or narcissistic in the way they expect others to fall in with their image of themselves. Those people who have a weak sense of themselves and their identity may engage in behaviour that is self-abusive. Or they may suffer from schizophrenia, where they experience themselves as so free and undefined that they are easily overcome by others and lose their bearings (Deurzen, 2010). This illustrates the importance of a selfhood that is both open and questioning and capable of affirmation and self-validation. As always, the objective is that of flexibility and dynamic balance.

The aim for clients in the personal dimension is then to gain a greater understanding of their identity and where they are on the polarities of this dimension, but also to understand that their identity is not fixed, that they are capable of change, and indeed do change constantly and continuously. This may result in a person discovering just how flexible they are and how creative they can be in thinking about themselves, in recognising their talents, characteristics and special qualities, whilst at the same time being open to adapt to different contexts, situations and experiences.

24

Living in the world spiritually

Beyond our physical, social and personal experience is another dimension of understanding, which comes from a more intuitive perception of the overall meaning of existence. This final dimension of human existence is often referred to as the spiritual dimension. The use of the term 'spiritual' might suggest that this dimension has a religious aspect. Indeed, some of the existential philosophers, such as Kierkegaard (1844) and Buber (1929), were particularly interested in how we connected and related to God. However, the spiritual dimension is not only confined to our relationship with God. It concerns our relationship to something beyond us, something trans personal: an unknown metaphysical dimension, whether that is experienced as God or the universe, or something else. We could call it the philosophical or existential dimension as well.

The spiritual dimension is also the realm in which we make sense of the world and where we create meaning and purpose. It is the dimension of our values and beliefs, which in turn informs our assumptions about the world. It is where our personal values and beliefs intersect with the world and where we put our lives into perspective. As shown in Chapter 14, our values and beliefs orientate us in the world. They will determine our attitudes towards the world and others. Quite often we inherit values and beliefs from our parents, or from the people we surround ourselves with; without explicitly taking on board what they mean for us and the way we live our lives, we kind of just soak the ideas up. But when certain unexpected events shake up our settled lives and take away the habitual ideas that we had taken for granted, we may come to realise that we have to work out how things actually fit together and what our lives are about. It is, therefore, in moments of crisis that we start to re-evaluate what we believe in. When life becomes difficult, it is sometimes because our values and beliefs are out of line with our experiences or clash with each other. Through existential therapy clients are able to see that there may be other ways of making sense of the world, that the values and beliefs they hold on to so tightly can be adapted and changed to be more in tune with the life they are living. This will often call for a re-evaluation of who they think they are in terms of their personal identity. But it also involves some thinking about the project of their life, and the meaning of their existence, and will frequently lead to a change of direction.

The spiritual dimension is orientated towards the future – it points to our ideal world. It is the dimension from which we project ourselves forward. It is where we connect to our original project (Sartre, 1943). Thinking about our lives at this level involves us in uncovering our motivations and aspirations. In the process of connecting to the future and our aspirations, we will set goals for ourselves, things to strive towards and achieve, but it will also involve a change in our mentality, our intentionality towards the world. Clients will often come to therapy because they have lost their sense of purpose, and the motivation needed to live more fulfilling lives. The energy or life force needed to propel ourselves forward – that is needed to find the courage to be (Tillich, 1952) – is created in the spiritual dimension and can only be accessed if we are willing to face the troubles of life that challenge us.

This dimension is about meaning and therefore the most important aspects of work done at this level are in relation to how we find, discover, distil or create meaning. As we have seen, Frankl (1946) saw meaning as a fundamental aspect of human existence. He said that we can either find meaning in the things we take from the world (experiential values) or in the things that we contribute to the world (creative values), or if neither of these is possible, in how we create value when everything becomes seemingly impossible. This is about facing our suffering when meaning is lost (attitudinal values). Clients often discover this through the difficulties they are facing: troubles show them the way towards meaning. Tillich spoke of existential courage as the capacity to affirm one's being in the face of non-being. And this paradox is precisely the tension we struggle with at this dimension.

These are the questions that we will all struggle with. How can we create a personally meaningful life, despite boredom, hardship, losses and limitations? Of course, all of this is negotiated within the context of our relationships at the other dimensions. We can only gain understanding of the whole picture of our lives to the extent we are gaining an understanding of ourselves in the personal dimension, of our relationships in the social dimension and of our embodiment in the physical world around us. The spiritual dimension is where these other dimensions are brought together and where we get a holistic perspective on how it all fits together. It is from this basis that we are able to find purpose, to be motivated and allow inspiration to take hold of us. Purpose and meaning come from our capacity to see all the connections and put the pieces of the puzzle together to come to a picture that coheres and makes sense.

The polarity that is experienced in this dimension is about our struggle with good and evil. It is about our moral struggle to live our lives in the best way possible. As we live life, we gradually gain a sense of what we believe is good and what we strive towards, on the one hand, and, on the other hand, we recognise beliefs, actions and ideologies that we consider wrong and that feel destructive or evil. We need to find our place within this polarity. Not everything we are and do is good. As soon as we affirm ourselves and take action, we make mistakes and can become a problem to somebody or something else. Our values and beliefs will help us determine what we experience as right and good, and we may find guidance on our path by creating a strong moral and ethical compass. But we will often have to discover that nothing is quite so black and white, and we need to learn to weigh up the consequences of different sets of actions, none of which is simply good or evil. We need to learn to live with a certain amount of ambiguity and flexibility. A further polarity of this dimension is that of being and nothingness. We constantly try to hang on to being and fill our time in the best way possible, and yet we are constantly reminded of nothingness as well. Having to create and re-create ourselves, on the one hand, and facing a sense of annihilation, on the other, constitute an ever-repeated challenge for all of us. It is important to often pause for thought to allow ourselves to understand this.

The difficulties that people face on this dimension are linked to the extent to which they hold on dogmatically to their convictions. If we hold a very narrow and definite view, we will experience a great deal more friction than if we can have a broader perspective that is truth finding and searching instead of affirmative of one particular angle. Strongly held values and beliefs can turn to zeal and fanaticism. A lack of direction and purpose may be experienced as dullness, negativity or apathy. Some clients may feel so passionate about their beliefs that they experience such moments as manic. At other times they may feel so disenchanted with reality that they give up and become listless, despairing or depressed. People who isolate themselves through their beliefs may end up becoming paranoid about being persecuted by others who are in disagreement. Most people struggle to some extent with the creation of a vision of life that is both inspired and yet realistic. If we give up on this battle for meaning, we typically end up lacking in purpose and motivation. For people in that situation, life may seem to have deserted them; it may appear bleak and pointless.

This dimension is about our search for truth and wisdom and requires us to fundamentally tackle how we create meaningful lives for ourselves. We have to do this in the face of a lack of certainty and with the constant threat of attacks on our safety and being. We are limited in time, and the challenge of making something worthwhile in a finite life that may initially seem absurd is not an easy proposition (Camus, 1942). There are many ways in which we can take up the challenge of human existence. For this we need existential courage, so that we can turn tragedies into triumphs and find meaning in our suffering (Frankl, 1946).

25

The emotional world of the client

Emotions act as our personal built-in compass; they orientate us and give us information about our connection with the world. What makes the existential approach to emotions distinctive is that emotions are not viewed as being either positive or negative. There are no value judgements placed on the type of emotion that a client feels. Instead, the existential approach focuses on recognising the importance of emotions and on understanding how they connect to the values in our lives.

Existential philosophers have always been interested in emotions. Heidegger (1927) talked about them in terms of mood, or *Stimmung*, which means the way we are tuned to the world, or the mood we are in. Moods express our attunement to the world. They tell us how and where we find ourselves (*Befindlichkeit*). Heidegger observed that, in the same way in which there is always weather, we are always in a mood and, therefore, we can only ever replace one mood with another. We cannot stop being in a mood. Therefore, the existential approach does not seek to suppress or get rid of emotions; instead it focuses on understanding what each emotion is telling us about the situation we find ourselves in. For Sartre (1962), however, emotions took on a magical quality. He believed that our pre-reflective emotional responses help us to cope with whatever we are facing, by transforming the world. Emotion does not happen in isolation. It is always connected *to* something; it is part of our intentionality towards the world. Emotion is our response to the world and, as Strasser (1999) stated, emotions constantly reveal our worldview. Sartre spoke about active emotions: allowing ourselves to reach for certain experiences rather than others by situating ourselves in relation to the world in a deliberate rather than reactive manner, and acting accordingly.

Working with emotions

When working with emotions the existential therapist often makes use of the emotional compass, devised by van Deurzen (2010, 2012; Deurzen and Adams, 2016) and reproduced in Figure 25.1, to help clients gain a deeper understanding of their feelings and how these emotions move and change direction. Emotions and feelings are not straightforward and often cannot be easily isolated and defined. Clients may feel a mix of emotions or may be unsure what emotion they are feeling or in relation to what. Or clients will feel taken over by their emotions and at their mercy. The existential therapist will first help the client to try to recognise what it is that they are feeling, to tease out, by asking clients to give examples, what the feelings are and what these emotions are connected to. Emotions always connect to our values: they are our way of moving out of ourselves (e-mote) towards a world. We either move towards a value in an up-swing of emotion, or we move away from a value in a down-swing of emotion. On the emotional compass the Magnetic North at the top represents the value of the client. Being united with our values makes us happy and makes us feel high, literally on top of the world. The bottom of the compass represents the absence of our value and makes us feel low, literally at rock bottom.

Using the emotional compass, the therapist can help the client to recognise and name the emotions that they are feeling, but also to see how these emotions express their particular position in relation to their owned, or lost, value. The emotional compass is held on an axis and we have already looked at the two extreme positions at the top and the bottom that represent polar opposites. But all other emotions also come in pairs. So, the opposite of jealousy (where I try to hold on to my value) is envy (where I want a value that is not mine yet). If the client is in the eastern hemisphere, their emotions are leading from happiness towards loss and depression. Feelings of pride are the first step down from the happiness we feel over ownership of something that is valued. In feeling pride we distance ourselves from our value by objectifying it and move one step towards the loss of that value. Jealousy is the next step down and is the feeling of vigilance of trying to keep hold of our value, when it is under threat. Anger comes next, when we slip away from our value and summon up the energy to fight to retain it. Fear follows that, when we feel so under threat at the attack on our value that we just want to abandon it and run away in self-protection. Sorrow follows that, when we have become aware that we have lost our value. As we slip down the right side of the compass, we become more and more disengaged with the things that are of value in our life and therefore we become isolated and despairing. It is the lower region in which we feel we have lost something meaningful. Often this feeling is not articulated or understood in relation to its valued lost object.

If clients are in the western hemisphere of the compass, they are in an upward movement towards something they want and treasure. At first, they traverse the negativity of guilt and shame, as they still doubt that they can achieve their value. Then they become more engaged, reconnecting with their aspirations and goals and gaining something that they feel is worthy. The emotions then go upwards from envy and longing to active hope and then to the commitment

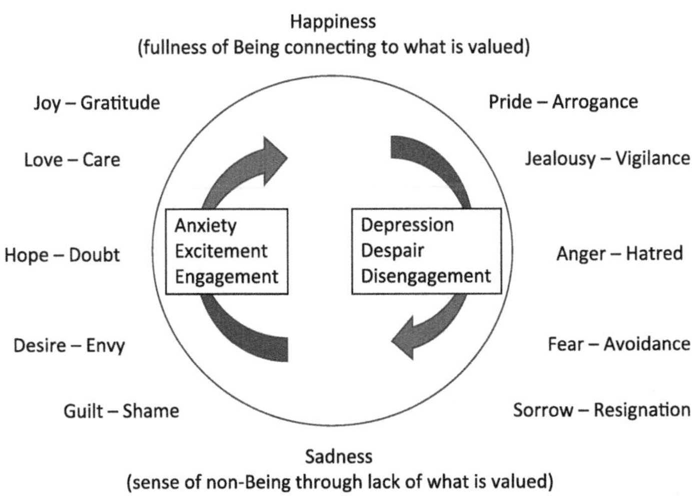

Figure 25.1 Emotional compass

and hard work of love, until we arrive at the joy of achieving our value where we feel a sudden sense of belonging and possession of what is good. We now come back to the top, where we are happy about being united with what we value, but of course we shall always start sliding away from it again. The cycle of emotions happens on many different levels and in relation to many valued objectives, often all at the same time.

Existential therapists enable clients to understand the meaning and message of their emotions and the values they point to. They do not teach control over or management of emotions but encourage clients to discover what their emotions tell them about their situation. This brings clarity and gives them mastery and self-understanding.

Case illustration – Jenny

Jenny was a mother of two small children who sought therapy because she felt angry all the time and it was affecting her relationship with her children. To start with, the therapist asked Jenny to describe the situations which made her feel angry. As she started to do this, she realised that each individual event was not really that bad and didn't warrant her outburst of emotion. But it seemed that the culmination of all these individual events meant that the overriding feeling of anger and frustration was very near the surface and would get triggered by the smallest thing. On further exploration Jenny was able to see that in each of her examples there was a theme of not being listened to, of events feeling out of her control despite the way she was trying so hard. It left her feeling that she wasn't being the mother she wanted to be. Being a good mum was her objective, her value, and it seemed to be taken from her time and time again. This led into a discussion of what being a mother meant to her, what aspects were important to her and what she valued about it. In the process Jenny came to understand how much she wanted to be playful and loved and liked by her children, but was losing the very thing she valued by becoming so irritable and resentful. Armed with this new understanding, Jenny was able to become more flexible in how she saw herself and found new ways of making sense of her situation and responding in playful ways that made her able to live and be more creatively as a mother. This gradually built and allowed her to shape her world to become much more like what she aspired to.

26

Embodiment

Our existence begins in a physical and bodily way, as we burst forth into the world, at birth. Undoubtedly there is some physical awareness even in the womb, but as we are born we become exposed to the physical world around us and survival becomes a vital issue. The importance of our bodily existence is experienced by babies in a sequence of new discoveries as they slowly come to explore themselves. May (1973) illustrated that when a baby grasps her own leg, she gets a sense of 'that is me'. We are embodied beings and it is through our bodies that we experience the world but also ourselves. Merleau-Ponty (1962) was one of the first existential philosophers to emphasise the role of the body in our existence and to address the Cartesian split, introduced by Descartes (1968), between mind and body. He showed how we always are both touched by the world and touching the world. Our embodiment is always ambiguous. Instead of a split, there is intertwining. Although Nietzsche (1883), Sartre (1943), Heidegger (1927) and Marcel (1964) have all stressed that the body is not something that I have, but rather something *that I am*, Merleau-Ponty argued that perception of the world is only possible through our bodies, and that embodiment involves the world as much as it involves us. For Merleau-Ponty our bodily experience, or embodiment, cannot be separated from our experience of being. Our emotions are biologically felt and expressed by our bodies, so that we think with our bodies. Meaning is created through our bodies in a sensory way, and our bodies don't just take up space in the world but rather respond and interact with the environment around us (Diamond, 1996). In the same way, our experience of others and the world is mediated through our body. Even the process of touching another involves at the same time the feeling of being touched by the other in return, which Merleau-Ponty termed reversibility.

Tuning into our bodily experience

Emotions, as the previous chapter demonstrated, can help us to navigate our experience of life. They give us information about how we feel in any given situation and they tell us what it is that truly matters to us. However, it is not always clear to people how they feel, particularly if they haven't developed a way of recognising or naming their emotional experiences. Working with the body is a way of transcending this lack of awareness and language, as we can begin by becoming more aware of our five senses and the state of our body. May (1973) noted that when we ask the question 'how do I feel right now?', we instantly turn our attention inwards and connect to our bodily experience and our senses. This has a dual effect. Firstly, the question focuses on the individual, the 'I' of the question, so that I am active in the feeling and recognise that this feeling belongs to me. Secondly, the question makes us focus on the here and now, how I feel right now in this moment. May believed that we need to become more aware of our bodies and to listen to what our bodies are telling us. He stated that 'it is not the attitude of "My *body* feels" but "*I* feel" (May, 1973: 109) that we need to encourage, particularly with our clients. This bodily attunement might involve recognising the pleasure we might take in eating, savouring the texture and flavour of the food. It will also involve an awareness of everything that hurts or upsets us and may lead to an understanding of how our posture and gestures mould to that experience. This kind of attunement work was a central part of encounter groups, is central to the phenomenologically based method of focusing and has been rediscovered in the currently popular practice of mindfulness.

However, Bugental (1981) warns that awareness of our embodiment also evokes anxiety. Embodiment is an existential given and it alerts us to our vulnerability. We therefore tend to suppress feelings of pain which may feel dangerous or destructive. Unfortunately, this suppression often means that we repress other feelings, such as joy and pleasure, as well. Thus, our emotional and bodily experience gets dampened down and we may become detached and apathetic. May (1969), whose work on Daimonic forces is echoed in Bugental's

(1981) and Schneider and May's (1995) ideas, believed that clients need space within the therapeutic relationship to retrieve and freely express these painful experiences.

Eugene Gendlin – focusing

Gendlin, inspired by existential-phenomenology, was particularly interested in what he termed 'experiencing', which referred to the 'flow of feeling' (Gendlin, 1962: 3). Experiencing is constant and occurs in every moment of behaviour and thought. How we experience a situation will involve an interaction between the person and the environment or the world of others. Gendlin showed that focusing on experiencing in the therapeutic relationship enabled change for clients. For Gendlin the 'felt sense', i.e. the bodily response to experience, was more important than emotional attunement. He also emphasised the link between language and embodiment as being crucial to express our bodily experience in order to discover and create meaning.

Working with embodiment

Helping clients to become more attuned to their embodiment involves turning their attention inwards by asking them how they feel in their body. For example:

Client:	I feel anxious when I am in social situations.
Therapist:	Where do you feel that anxiety in your body?
Client:	In my chest. I feel my chest becoming really tight and I begin to worry that I won't be able to breathe.
Therapist:	What is that like to feel your chest tighten?
Client:	I can feel my heart beating faster and my breathing is quicker, and I start feeling faint – I need to escape, run away, quickly before anyone sees.

An example of focusing in the above illustration would be to invite the client to sit with that feeling of anxiety in order to get her to understand it by embodying it fully. We might say: ‘Would it be ok to just let yourself feel that, the way it is in that situation, while you are sitting here with me?’; ‘What word would you use to describe that feeling?’ (Madison, 2010: 196). Madison states that *living* that bodily experience in the session is more important than the content of the experience. He believes that therapists often miss opportunities to allow the felt experience to be explored more fully in the session. Existential therapists include work with embodiment in the wide range of their practice.

27

Examining the paradoxes of life

Life is not straightforward; it is complicated and full of contradictions. Our lives are filled with tensions and paradoxes; some we are able to tolerate but others can cause us anxiety and leave us feeling unsettled. This is why we often deny one aspect of a conflict, or a dilemma, focusing on either the positive or the negative. Most clients come to therapy in order to resolve a conundrum that they are facing. Often this will be when clients' dilemmas begin to have an adverse effect on their lives. They may be struggling with their social relationships, for example, or wish to feel happier or more content, and it may seem to them that their present way of living is stopping them doing that. Clients bring the paradoxes that they are facing to therapy and often present them as a conflict or problem that needs to be solved, as if they have an either/or choice. However, paradoxes cannot be solved in this way. As we have seen in earlier chapters, human existence involves us being caught up in the tensions of paradox. Life itself is a constant tension and interplay between love and hate, closeness and isolation, strength and weakness, meaning and absurdity, freedom and necessity. If we think of each paradox as having opposing poles at either end of a spectrum, then we will be able to see how we continuously oscillate between these two extremes. Our aim is not to settle at one end or the other. Life is mediated by movement: it is onto-dynamic. Therefore, we cannot solve paradoxes by choosing one pole over the other. Instead existential therapists will involve their clients in a dialectical discussion. When we talk about life, we always have to consider its opposite, death, as both are contained within the experience of being human. Each is defined in relation to the other. We cannot have one without the other. We have to consider both the thesis and the antithesis, as together they form a whole (Deurzen and Adams, 2016). By considering both poles of existence, and the relationship between them, we come to understand our predicament in a new way. We see that it is only in mastering the movement at each dimension of life that we become flexible enough to transcend our issues. In the social dimension clients often struggle with the tension between being too isolated and feeling too close or merged with others. Both sides need to be faced, explored and understood before clients can find their own position in this paradox and learn to overcome their problems with this conundrum by learning how to move between these poles in a playful way. This is not to say that their new position will become fixed, but rather that they will become more creative in the way they view the inevitable paradoxes and tensions that they face. It simply is part of being human. Recognising that there will be times when they want to separate from others and be alone and other times when they want to connect to others more fully will help them learn how to manage both ways of relating.

Working with paradox

Deurzen stresses the importance of working with paradox in therapy: 'Paradox and passion are the bedrock and fuel of our work and it is by opening ourselves to their full impact on the client that new purpose can be generated and sustained' (Deurzen, 1998: 3). Existential therapists will therefore look out for their clients' either/or statements. Where they relate to the paradoxical nature of existence, they will often introduce the subject as a conflict or a choice. Of course, clients are not always aware of the paradoxes that they are facing and therefore therapists will make more explicit what has been implicitly expressed by the client. We aim to help clients to reformulate their concerns as something that is both/and rather than something that is either/or. In this way problems will no longer seem like un-overcomable conflicts but will be experienced as challenges. People will soon learn to transcend what seems like an opposition and translate this new understanding into a more fluid way of existing.

Case illustration – Julian

Julian came to therapy because he wanted to leave his girlfriend of five years. He had not been happy for some time but also found that he was not finding it easy to leave the life he had built with her. Julian felt that therapy would help him solve this question of whether he would stay or leave.

The therapy explored all the things that were wrong with the relationship; these were all too easy for him to detail and list. However, the existential therapist also asked Julian to examine all that was good in the relationship too. This, Julian found, was a lot harder to do. At first, he didn't allow himself to consider what might be good and what he might miss, if he left. It was as if somehow it would undermine his resolve to leave. Through a dialectical discussion with the therapist, Julian found he could hold both, the good and the bad, in the relationship. By taking on board both poles of the experience he was able to get a deeper understanding of his relationship. He discovered that what made it good were the intimacy and closeness with his partner and their shared history. But also he was now able to pinpoint that what he struggled with was feeling neglected, in constant disagreement and often a lack of communication. Julian began to see how these things were happening. This allowed him to track his part in the relationship too and how he might contribute to the things that were wrong with it. Rather than making an either/or choice, Julian gained a new understanding of himself and what he wanted from the relationship. This new understanding had an impact on how he thought and how he related to his partner. By facing the paradoxical nature of his relationship and his own contradictory desires for closeness and distance, Julian was able to find a new way of relating and this helped him to create a more fruitful way of being with his partner. He accepted his paradox by recognising that relationships are full of contradictions. He was able to leave his old way of being behind and to stay with his girlfriend.

Using the four worlds

Paradoxes appear on every level of existence. By using the four worlds model, existential therapists can help clients locate and understand the paradoxes that they face. This is specifically useful for helping clients to see the implicit paradoxes that all of us face, necessarily, on each dimension of existence. Often clients find it very reassuring to come to realise that life poses the same problems for all of us and that we can get better at handling these issues by facing them. Once we stop feeling guilty or silly about making mistakes, it becomes easier to bring new problems and solve them. The existential therapist will encourage clients to have the courage to face their struggles and predicaments head on. They will always support them to explore all facets of a situation and see both sides of a dilemma, in order to gain a deeper understanding of their life and the human condition.

28

Revisiting values and beliefs

As we have seen, our view of the world, the judgements we make and the opinions we hold and the assumptions we may not be aware of are all governed by our values and beliefs. These provide the structure and foundations for how we make sense of ourselves and the world. They develop in response to our experiences in life. However, sometimes we collect values and beliefs from people around us, go along with what they believe without really thinking whether that fits for us as individuals. A good example of this is how we may carry with us into our adult life the values and beliefs that our parents hold. The same might happen in our teenage years when we pick up new ideas, values and worldviews from our peers and take these on board unquestioningly.

Some values and beliefs are more transparent, more explicit and known to us as individuals. If a person has a strong religious belief, for example, they will take on the values and beliefs of that religion as it represents something that they stand for and will align themselves with. It is often difficult for such a belief to remain open to questioning and there is the risk of it becoming static and even dogmatic or, worse, fanatical. Some people may have political or ideological values, which will influence their beliefs about the society they live in and what they feel is important within that society. Dogmatism and fanaticism may also show up here and that is even the case if our beliefs are based on scientific ideas, for we may become so convinced of the accuracy of our factual data base that we forget to update it regularly.

However, there is another layer of value and belief that is more implicit. These ideas are formed through our interactions with others and the world. We may form beliefs about what to expect in certain situations or generalise our experience of an individual event to all.

For example, a person who was bitten by a dog as a child may hold the belief that all dogs are dangerous. Or clients may come to develop beliefs about themselves such as that they are not good in relationships, or that people will always bully them. These more implicit beliefs will have an impact on how they are in the world. The person who was bitten by a dog may avoid all dogs – even the friendly ones – and will therefore not have an opportunity to challenge their firmly held belief. The client who believes that everyone will bully them will enter all relationships with that expectation; they may play a passive or victim role rather than standing up for themselves, and seek out examples of interactions which will reinforce their belief. It is important for such erroneous beliefs to be challenged and for the person to be freed from such misconceptions about themselves, but this kind of insight usually comes slowly after experimentation and cannot be imposed by a therapist.

Working with values and beliefs

When we think carefully about our lives, we will see just how many beliefs influence how we live, even down to how many meals we have a day. Almost everything we do is governed by a value and a belief, and often these are related to moral judgements too. It is therefore really important to help clients become aware of what values and beliefs they do hold so that they can re-evaluate whether they are still applicable to their lives today. Our experiences and views change over time and yet we often hold on to old frames of reference. When this happens, clients find that they encounter problems, even though they obtain safety from sticking with these old views. In existential therapy, therapists will gently challenge clients on the beliefs they hold, asking them what makes that belief important to them and how it is connected to their values. In this way clients can scrutinise their beliefs and question themselves as to why they hold that belief, how it connects to their life and how relevant it is for them and their lives today. In this way the client gets a sense of what is really important. They can own the old beliefs and replace them with new findings if they want to. They discover what they do or do not want to change and where the flexibility lies – what is open to change. They also experience the permissiveness of the therapist who does not ridicule or force them into changing their views.

Case illustration – Steve

On the surface, Steve seemed to have a good life; he had always had good jobs in IT, which had paid well. He was in a long-term relationship and had a nice home. However, he had come to therapy because, despite his seemingly happy life, he didn't feel happy. Steve found his work meaningless. He despised the corporate environment that he worked in and felt that he was caught up in internal politics which had become soul destroying. Steve really wanted to do something more creative. He had always been drawn towards the natural world and wanted to live a simpler life with his girlfriend. However, he felt unable to make this move out of the corporate world into a more meaningful and creative endeavour.

As the therapy progressed, it became clear that the sticking point for Steve concerned his values and beliefs. The reality of living a more creative existence meant he would not earn as much money, and this in turn would mean that in his own eyes and by his personal standards he was not successful. Steve had a clear idea of what 'being successful' entailed, and he had, quite effectively, managed to create this kind of success for himself. On further exploration he established that these ideals of success had been handed down from his parents and been reinforced by expectations he had picked up from his wider social environment of friends and acquaintances. When he talked about the type of creative work he could undertake, he became quite excited and energised but was still overcome by fears about how others would judge him. Of course, it was more about how he was judging himself. Could he still be successful and not earn as much money? The therapy helped him to realise that in order to do this he needed to re-evaluate what success meant to him. He recognised that what he valued was doing meaningful work and that that was more important than the money he earned. So long as he was able to pay for the basics, then he would be OK. Steve started to see how living in this simpler way would be challenging; to survive on less money would take skill and cunning and he saw that success could be found in making this way of living work. Although there was still a long way to go for Steve, he felt that this shift in his values and beliefs meant that he could be more open to finding the type of work or the way of living that was more in line with what was important to him. As it turned out, his girlfriend found his decision to change his lifestyle very appealing and this led to both of them moving to the countryside. The important aspect of this change was that Steve felt he had arrived at his decision by taking the time to understand his own priorities and had then been able to discuss it all fully with his girlfriend. They owned the decision together and enjoyed the change when it came.

29

Making meaning and discovering purpose

We are now, in contemporary culture, more than ever seeking to understand ourselves better and find more meaningful ways of living – at least those of us who are fortunate enough to be able to afford this kind of reflective living. Clients who come to therapy are often in what Frankl (1967) describes as an 'Existential Vacuum'. They have lost their purpose, their motivation and their energy in life and feel that their lives are meaningless. They feel as if they have stagnated and experience a sense of stasis and disconnection, as it is meaning that links us to the world and propels us forward into our futures. For Frankl meaning has to be ahead of our existence: 'it sets the pace for being' (Frankl, 1967: 12).

Discovering meaning

For those clients who have lost a sense of meaning and purpose in their lives there is a need to reconnect to their lives and this is done by taking awareness of how they are living, what is important to them and what they value. All these aspects are contained within meaning. Meaning flows from our connectivity. It stems from the way in which we are connected and engaged with the fundamental aspects of who we are; it brings our values and beliefs together with our emotional response to the world. All these elements are needed to make sense of our present experiences as well as giving us a sense of direction in life.

Existential therapy, therefore, focuses on helping clients to discover meaning in their lives, both in terms of what words and situations actually signify to them and in terms of the search for an overall meaning of life. Meaning can be found in all situations and experiences if we orientate ourselves to discovering it. This discovery is similar to Heidegger's idea of disclosing, that the world discloses itself to us in a way that we are able to grasp and make sense of it. Discovering meaning may be difficult for clients who feel apathetic or find life pointless or empty. Helping clients to confront this kind of meaninglessness and the absurdity of life can help them connect with what they want to accomplish. It leads us to the ultimate question in life: how do we spend the limited time we have between birth and death? Deurzen (2012) argues that meaning is linked to our ultimate concerns (Jaspers, 1951; Yalom, 1980). When we face the limits of our existence, we paradoxically discover meaning because we are aware of what we may lose. Finding meaning is 'not to soothe one's conscience but to stir it up' (Frankl, 1967: 12). Camus, in the *Myth of Sisyphus*, said that we never find meaning despite difficulties and challenges, but because of them. What challenges us forces us to wake up, engage and connect, and connections are what create meaning.

Logotherapy

Frankl (1955, 1967, 1946) developed logotherapy, where *logos* denotes the Greek word for meaning, to assist clients to rediscover meaning in their lives. Through logotherapy clients are enabled to see how they create meaning by the way they act and experience the world – what they give and receive in life. We derive meaning from enjoying the things around us, the good things in our lives. But we also create meaning by adding to these things and contributing something to the world. Finally, we can find meaning in our own attitude towards the things that apparently rob us of meaning. The way we make our suffering purposeful is the utmost way of meaning making.

Therapists will help clients to highlight what types of experiences are important to them so that they can find ways of incorporating these meaningful things into their everyday lives. But they will also challenge clients' attitudes towards themselves and the world. Most particularly they will not take difficulties away or provide answers, but they will challenge their clients to find depth in their troubles and new purpose in their attempts at enduring and overcoming obstacles and crises. Making sense of the more difficult experiences is the ultimate way that Frankl showed us to transform our suffering into something of value. Recognising that, even in situations where we have no control, we do have control over our responses is paramount. For Frankl this ability to choose our attitude towards suffering enables clients to find meaning in that situation. Frankl believed that life contains a series of questions. Each situation asks something of us and we need to determine how we respond and in this way discover the meaning we give to each aspect of life. The meaning we find in those moments is individual to each of us and therefore the search for meaning is a personal struggle. Frankl noted that meaning relates to accepting the responsibility of our existence. We are asked a question and we need to answer to life: we are responsible for what we make of it. He devised a number of techniques to help clients to reconnect with meaning and become more response-able for their own existence.

Paradoxical Intention

Paradoxical Intention is used to help clients to confront the things they fear. If a client fears she will faint when she is in a crowd of people, then the logotherapist would encourage that client to seek out crowded places and to try to imagine she wished to intentionally faint. When the client discovers that she has not fainted, she begins to see the situation in a new way; she has faced her fear and is beginning to play with her fate.

De-reflection

De-reflection is another technique to help clients move away from being overly preoccupied with themselves by distracting themselves from their difficulties with the world around them. Frankl (1955) gives the example of insomnia, where clients are encouraged to try to stay awake whilst lying in the dark, rather than focusing on their lack of sleep.

Logotherapy can be seen as being quite directive in its approach (Cooper, 2016) but at the same time it challenges clients to take responsibility for their lives. These techniques can be helpful when used in a humorous way and as part of an ongoing therapeutic relationship.

Socratic dialogue

Engaging clients in Socratic dialogue will also help them to clarify and understand how they create meaning, and particularly to uncover the creative, experiential and attitudinal values that they hold. Socratic dialogue consists of enabling a person to discover what they already know for themselves about something that they have thus far avoided reflecting on.

Case illustration – Michael

Michael was in a deep depression when he came to therapy. He felt a great wave of apathy, no motivation, and no will to do anything – life indeed had no meaning for him. He had effectively isolated himself and constricted his world so that his contact with other people and the outside world was very limited. The therapy focused on gaining an understanding of Michael's sense of himself and his world. He talked about how he had loved art as a child but had had to stop because his parents' focus was on more academic pursuits. Through discussing what art meant to him, Michael realised that this was a big regret in his life and wondered whether it was something he could pursue now that he was older. The therapist encouraged him to find ways to connect with the world and with other people, which eventually prompted him to enrol on an evening art course. Through this course he became reinvigorated, although it was difficult at first; he found a passion for drawing and painting which had lain dormant. Michael also started to build some friendships with others on the course and he began to feel more connected with others and therefore with himself. Through a process of Socratic dialogue with the therapist Michael was also able to challenge some of his sedimented attitudinal values and to begin to realise he was wiser than he thought and could see his life in a new way. Although it still felt limited in many ways, he realised that he was discovering what he valued and what was meaningful for him in his life. As his world expanded, so did his meaning and purpose, which helped him to think about new directions his life might take. It was the very freedom to change and explore things creatively that had become the most meaningful to Michael. This gladdened him greatly.

30

Finding freedom

Helping clients to find greater freedom is the ultimate aim of existential therapy. Together we work towards an understanding of the tensions, conflicts, dilemmas and paradoxes that are holding a person back. We seek to throw light where there was darkness, in order to liberate people and give them back to themselves where they felt alienated, and to reconnect them where they felt isolated. Each stage of existential therapy allows clients to look beyond their own particular view of the world and to begin to think about how they might view and experience their lives in different and more truthful ways.

Existential therapists will therefore:

- Encourage clients to describe their lives in great detail, eliciting descriptions of the way they relate to others, as well as the way in which they live their lives.
- Ask clients to take stock of where they are at present – how their working lives interact with their personal lives, how they see themselves and how they understand the difficulties that they experience.
- Explore the landscapes of the past that shaped their current situation and unearth some of the hidden treasures in these experiences that had been lost because of their present suffering.
- Get a sense of the future they are hoping for and contrast this with the future they fear they are rushing towards.
- Map these descriptions on to the four dimensions of existence, so that the therapist and client can gain a deeper understanding of which dimensions the clients have strengths in and where they experience struggle.
- Help clients to think about and clarify their values and beliefs, highlighting what is important to them and what opinions/

judgements/assumptions they hold in relation to the world and to other people. This may involve both challenge and acceptance.

- Check the meaning of what the client says, in terms of the examples they give and the words they use. Existential therapists will attempt to be as open as they can to what the client is saying and to understand the client from their perspective.
- In order to make sure we do this, we keep verifying whether our understanding matches the client's experience.
- Tune into the emotional flavour of the client's experience, to determine what the client's mood or emotion is telling the client about their interactions with the world.
- Help the client to focus on their bodily experience and what information their sensations are giving them about their present experience.
- Raise clients' awareness of how they live in time and the impact their temporality has on their experience of life and the way they respond to both past and present experiences, but also helping clients to think about how they are limited in time and what that limitation means in terms of their future.
- Make explicit the paradoxical nature of existence by highlighting the paradoxes that clients face and helping them to find a way of existing in the full range of human existence instead of by wishful thinking, avoidance or evasion.
- Explore meaning and meaninglessness with the client and enable them to discover the way in which they create and make meaning in their lives.
- Encourage clients to notice how they are making choices in their lives and how these choices impact on who they are and what they become, making active choices rather than passive ones.
- Encourage clients to think about themselves as having a dynamic sense of self rather than a static, object-like self.
- Enable each person to take back authority and stand their ground, with passion and compassion for others.
- Teach people to trust their intuition and feelings and create a habit of self-reflective awareness and communication both with self and other.

- Find the hope, the aspiration and the conviction that life is worth living and can have deep and important purpose.
- Inspire people with the sense that life is precious and that they have many yet unexploited abilities and talents to discover and hone.
- Free themselves from fears, bad memories and painful experiences, to find a new courage to face future challenges with confidence and commitment, intelligence and persistence.

Exploring each of the areas listed above will enable clients to start thinking about their lives in new ways and, more importantly, help them question how they are living their lives currently. It is only when we are able to question ourselves and our lives that we begin to see what is important and necessary. We become like scientists and researchers investigating our own existence. This allows us to start filtering experiences and feelings, letting go of some and allowing some to stay. This leads to flexibility. As soon as the client can see that there can be flexibility in how they think about themselves or how they relate to others, the possibility of freedom presents itself. We become free to choose our responses, at least to some extent. Freedom is only possible when we begin to take responsibility for ourselves. Accepting that who we are and how we live is to a large extent down to the choices we make or have made in the past is the first step towards liberation. Everything in life has to be chosen, including our outlook and our worldview, though initially we may just have fallen into these passively. Once clients are able to understand that they have this margin of freedom, they can begin to make more active and purposeful choices. Even small changes in how they perceive or process their world will have a big effect on their sense of themselves. They start to experiment. They are no longer passive victims but active participants. Each of the areas listed above involves a wide range of possibilities. Nothing is fixed in life; we are dynamic beings with the potential to alter and vary our views on who we are, how we think about past experiences, present predicaments and most importantly about what our future life could become. People can learn to use their imagination in a creative rather than in a destructive or despairing manner, and that makes all the difference between feeling down and disenfranchised or hopeful and engaged.

The distinctive features of existential therapy discussed in this text have shown our lives as created by our actions, interactions, experiences, emotions, sensations and reflections. All these interlinking aspects are interwoven and work together. Each facet of life is worth polishing and refining. All together they are like the faces of a prism, where each side represents the way in which we understand one aspect of existence. Their totality determines how we act and interact with our world. Depending on how we allow light to shine into the prisms of our lives, we will produce a different perspective. We can block out the light, we can distort it or we can refract it. We can also spread it and magnify it, if we make ourselves more transparent. How and where we shine that light is a choice that freedom offers us. Of course, it is not easy to accept our freedom and responsibility, as it causes us to feel existential anxiety. Sometimes it is easier to blame others or the situations we find ourselves in, but this will only ever lead to dissatisfaction and possibly despair. Facing our freedom and responsibility for our fate is a more difficult path in life, for which we need existential courage. When we accept this challenge, we create the potential for leading a more meaningful and purposeful life, where we will undoubtedly struggle and suffer but will also discover much that is of value and worth. Existential therapy seeks to return ownership of life to a person and to enable each to reclaim their authority over what they decide to make of the opportunities available to them. There are few things more satisfying than to acquire mastery over the time that has been given to us and to use it to the best of our abilities, making the most of who we are capable of being.

References

Aristotle (1976) *The Ethics of Aristotle*. Transl. J. A. K. Thomson. Harmondsworth: Penguin Books Ltd.

Binswanger, L. (1946) 'The Existential School of Thought'. Transl. E. Angel. In R. May, E. Angel and H. F. Ellenberger (eds.) *Existence*. New York: Basic Books. (1958).

Boss, M. (1963) *Psychoanalysis and Daseinsanalysis*. Transl. L. E. Lefebre. New York: Basic Books.

Boss, M. (1979) *Existential Foundations of Medicine and Psychology*. Transl. S. Conway and A. Cleaves. Northvale, NJ: Jason Aronson Inc.

Brentano, F. (1874) *Psychology from an Empirical Standpoint*. Abingdon: Routledge Classics. (2015).

Buber, M. (1929) *I and Thou*. Transl. R. G. Smith. New York: Scribner Classics. (1958).

Bugental, J. F. T. (1981) *The Search for Authenticity: An Existential-Analytic Approach to Psychotherapy*. New York: Irvington.

Camus, A. (1942) *The Myth of Sisyphus*. Harmondsworth: Penguin. (1975).

Cohn, H. W. (1997) *Existential Thought and Therapeutic Practice: An Introduction to Existential Psychotherapy*. London: Sage Publications.

Cooper, M. (2016) *Existential Therapies*. 2nd edition. London: Sage Publications. (2003).

Correia, E. A., Cooper, M. and Berdondini, L. (2016) Existential Therapy Institutions Worldwide: An Update of Data and the Extensive List. *Existential Analysis*, 27(1), pp. 155–197.

De Beauvoir, S. (1948) *The Ethics of Ambiguity*. New York: Citadel Press Books.

Descartes, R. (1968) *Discourse on Method and the Meditations*. London: Penguin Classics.

Deurzen, E. van (1988) *Existential Counselling in Practice*. 1st edition. London: Sage Publications.

Deurzen, E. van (1997) *Everyday Mysteries: Existential Dimensions of Psychotherapy*. 1st edition. London: Routledge.

Deurzen, E. van (1998) *Paradox and Passion in Psychotherapy: An Existential Approach.* Chichester: John Wiley & Sons Ltd. (2015).

Deurzen, E. van (2002) *Existential Counselling and Psychotherapy in Practice.* 2nd edition. London: Sage Publications.

Deurzen, E. van (2010) *Everyday Mysteries: Handbook of Existential Psychotherapy*. 2nd edition. London: Routledge.

Deurzen, E. van (2012) *Existential Counselling and Psychotherapy in Practice.* 3rd edition. London: Sage Publications.

Deurzen, E. van and Adams, M. (2011) *Skills in Existential Counselling and Psychotherapy*. 1st edition. London: Sage.

Deurzen, E. van and Adams, M. (2016) *Skills in Existential Counselling and Psychotherapy*. 2nd edition. London: Sage.

Deurzen, E. van and Arnold-Baker, C. (eds.) (2005) *Existential Perspectives on Human Issues: A Handbook for Therapeutic Practice*. Basingstoke: Palgrave Macmillan.

Diamond, N. (1996) Embodiment. *Journal of the Society for Existential Analysis,* 7(1), pp. 129–133.

Donne, J. (1624) *Devotions upon Emergent Occasions: Meditation 17*. New York: Vintage Spiritual Classics. (1999).

Einstein, A. (1961) *Relativity: The Special and General Theory*. Transl. R. W. Lawson. New York: Henry Holt and Company.

Ellenberger, H. F. (1958) 'A Clinical Introduction to Psychiatric Phenomenology and Existential Analysis'. In R. May, E. Angel and H. F. Ellenberger (eds.) *Existence*. New York: Basic Books. (1946, 1958).

Frankl, V. E. (1946) *Man's Search for Meaning*. New York: Washington Square Press. (1984).

Frankl, V. E. (1955) *The Doctor and the Soul: From Psychotherapy to Logotherapy*. Transl. A. A. Knopf. Harmondsworth: Penguin.

Frankl, V. E. (1967) *Psychotherapy and Existentialism: Selected Papers on Logotherapy*. London: Souvenir Press.

Gendlin, E. (1962) *Experiencing and the Creation of Meaning: A Philosophical and Psychological Approach to the Subjective*. Evanston, IL: Northwestern University Press.

Harris, M. A., Brett, C. E., Johnson, W. and Deary, I. J. (2016) Personality Stability from Age 14 to Age 77 Years. *Psychology and Aging*, 31(8), pp. 862–874.

Heidegger, M. (1927) *Being and Time*. Transl. J. Macquarrie and E. S. Robinson 1962. London: Harper and Row.

Heidegger, M. (1996) *Being and Time*. Transl. J. Stambaugh. Albany: State University of New York Press.

Hume, D. (1739) *A Treatise of Human Nature*. Oxford: Clarendon Press. (2014).

Husserl, E. (1900) *Logical Investigations*. Transl. J. N. Findlay. London: Routledge. (1970).

Husserl, E. (1985) *Origin and Development of Husserl's Phenomenology*. In *Encyclopaedia Britannica*, vol. 25, 15th edition. Chicago, IL.

Jaspers, K. (1951) *The Way to Wisdom*. Transl. R. Manheim. New Haven, CT, and London: Yale University Press.

Kant, I. (1922) *Critique of Pure Reason*. Transl. F. Max Meuller. New York: Macmillan and Co.

Kearney, R. (1994) *Modern Movements in European Philosophy*. Manchester: Manchester University Press.

Kierkegaard, S. (1843a) *Fear and Trembling*. Princeton, NJ: Princeton University Press. (1954).

Kierkegaard, S. (1843b) *Either/Or*, vols. I, II. Princeton, NJ: Princeton University Press. (1959).

Kierkegaard, S. (1844) *The Concept of Anxiety*. Transl. R. Thomte. Princeton, NJ: Princeton University Press. (1980).

Kierkegaard, S. (1849) *The Sickness unto Death*. Transl. H. V. Hong. Princeton, NJ: Princeton University Press. (1968).

Konstan, D. (2016) 'Epicurus'. In Edward N. Zalta (ed.) *Stanford Encyclopedia of Philosophy* (Fall 2016 edition), available at https://plato.stanford.edu/archives/fall2016/entries/epicurus/ (accessed 12 Jan. 2018).

Laing, R. D. (1959) *The Divided Self*. Harmondsworth: Penguin. (1970).

Locke, J. (1689) *Two Treatises of Government*. P. Laslett (ed.). Cambridge: Cambridge University Press. (1988).

Macaro, A. (2005) Aristotle and the Good Life. *Practical Philosophy*, Autumn, pp. 4–6.

Madison, G. (2010) Focusing on Existence: Five Facets of an Experiential-Existential Model. *Person-Centred and Experiential Psychotherapies*, 9(3), pp. 189–204

Marcel, G. (1964) *Creative Fidelity*. Transl. R. Rosthal. New York: Farrar, Strauss and Company.

May, R. (1969) *Love and Will*. New York: Norton.

May, R. (1973) *Man's Search for Himself*. New York: Dell Publishing.

May, R. (1983) *The Discovery of Being: Writings in Existential Psychology*. New York: W. W. Norton.

May, R., Angel, E., and Ellenberger, H. F. (1946) *Existence*. New York: Basic Books. (1958).

Merleau-Ponty, M. (1962) *Phenomenology of Perception*. Transl. C. Smith. London and New York: Routledge.

Minkowski, E. (1933) 'Findings in a Case of Schizophrenic Depression'. Transl. B. Bliss. In R. May, E. Angel and H. F. Ellenberger (eds.) *Existence*. New York: Basic Books. (1946, 1958).

Mulhall, S. (1996) *Heidegger and Being and Time*. London and New York: Routledge.

Mullen, J. D. (1995) *Kierkegaard's Philosophy: Self-Deception and Cowardice in the Present Age*. Lanham, MD: University Press of America, Inc.

Nietzsche, F. (1882) *The Gay Science*. Transl. W. Kaufmann. New York: Vintage Books. (1974).

Nietzsche, F. (1883) *Thus Spoke Zarathustra*. Transl. R. J. Hollingdale. Harmondsworth: Penguin. (1961).

Nietzsche, F. (1895) *The Will to Power*. Transl. W. Kaufmann and R. J. Hollingdale. New York: Vintage Books.

Nietzsche, F. (1977) *A Nietzsche Reader*. Transl. R. J. Hollingdale. Harmondsworth: Penguin.

Norcross, J. C. (2002) 'Empirically Supported Therapy Relationships'. In J. C. Norcross (ed.) *Psychotherapy Relationships That Work: Therapist Contributions and Responsiveness to Patients*. New York: Oxford University Press, pp. 3–16.

Plato (1871) *The Republic*. Transl. B. Jowett. New York: Vintage Books. (1991).

Plato (1966) *Plato in Twelve Volumes*, vol. 1. Transl. H. N. Fowler. Cambridge, MA: Harvard University Press.

Pollard, J. (2005) 'Authenticity and Inauthenticity'. In E. van Deurzen and C. Arnold-Baker (eds.) *Existential Perspectives on Human Issues: A Handbook for Therapeutic Practice*. Basingstoke: Palgrave Macmillan.

Sartre, J.-P. (1938) *Nausea*. Transl. Robert Baldick. Penguin: Harmondsworth. (1965).
Sartre, J.-P. (1943) *Being and Nothingness: An Essay on Phenomenological Ontology*. Transl. H. Barnes. New York: Phil. Library.
Sartre, J.-P. (1962) *Sketch for a Theory of the Emotions*. Transl. P. Mairet. London: Routledge.
Schneider, K. J. and May, R. (eds.) (1995) *The Psychology of Existence*. New York: McGraw-Hill.
Spinelli, E. (2002) *The Interpreted World: An Introduction to Phenomenological Psychology*. London: Sage Publications.
Strasser, F. (1999) *Emotions: Experiences in Existential Psychotherapy and Life*. Trowbridge: Duckworth Publishers.
Strasser, F. & Strasser, A. (1997) *Existential Time-Limited Therapy: The Wheel of Existence*. Chichester: John Wiley and Sons.
Szasz, T. (1961) *The Myth of Mental Illness*. New York: Harper.
Tarnas, R. (1991) *The Passion of the Western Mind: Understanding the Ideas That Have Shaped Our World View*. London: Random House.
Tillich, P. (1952) *The Courage to Be*. Glasgow: Penguin Classics.
von Uexküll, J. (1921) *Umwelt und Innenwelt der Tiere*. Berlin: J. Springer.
Warnock, M. (1970) *Existentialism*. Oxford: Oxford University Press.
Yalom, I. D. (1980) *Existential Psychotherapy*. New York: Basic Books.

Index

absurdity 13
Adams, M. 108
ambiguity 45–6
ancient philosophy 6–8, 45, 65, 68
anxiety 13–14, 37–41, 100
Aristotle 65, 68
assumptions 84 *see also* bias; values
authenticity 41–3, 53–5, 101
awareness 13–14, 68, 114 *see also* authenticity

being-for-others 20–1
being-in-the-world 12, 16–17
being-there 15–18
being-towards-death 57–8
being-with 19–20, 88
beliefs *see* values
bias 80–1
Binswanger, L. 87–9
body 91–3, 113–16
Boss, M. 87
Brentano, F. 27–8
Buber, M. 21, 76–7, 103
Bugental, J. F. T. 114–15

call of conscience 54–5
Camus, A. 13, 58, 126
care/concern 17, 24, 61–2
change 83
choice 33–5, 41, 133
classical philosophy *see* ancient philosophy
cognitive behavioural therapy 6
collaboration 22
communication 96
contradictions *see* paradoxes

Dasein see being-there
de Beauvoir, S. 35, 46
de-reflection 127–8
death 39, 46–7
Descartes, R. 113
description 79–80
determinism 33
Deurzen, E. van 29, 34, 39, 45, 76, 84, 93, 108, 118, 126
dialectic of time (DoT) 26
dimensions of existence *see* four dimensions of existence
Donne, J. 19
dynamic self *see* self

eidetic reduction 73
Eigenwelt see personal dimension
Einstein, A. 23
Ellenberger, H. F. 23
embodiment 91–3, 113–16
emotional compass 108–10
emotions 97, 107–11
enquiry 6–7
Epicurus 66
epoché 73
equalisation 81–2
eternal 38, 50, 67
ethics 65–6, 105 *see also* values
existential anxiety 38
existential guilt 41–3, 54–5, 100
experience 79, 115
explanation 79

fallenness 20, 54
finite 23, 38, 50
focusing 115
four dimensions of existence 89–90, 120; personal 49–52, 99–102; physical 91–4, 113–16; social 5, 19–22, 95–7; spiritual 103–6
Frankl, V. E. 59–60, 104, 125–8
freedom 13, 33, 131–4

Gendlin, E. 115
good life *see* living
guilt *see* existential guilt

Heidegger, M. 14, 95, 113; authenticity 55, 101; being-in-the-world 12, 16–17; being-there 15–18; being-towards-death 57–8; being-with 19–20, 88; care/concern 17, 24, 61–2; death anxiety 39; existential guilt 41–2, 54–5; fallenness 20, 54; intentionality 29; moods 107; self 51; the-They 20, 53–4; thrownness 17–18, 24; time 23–6
holism 5, 15, 17–18, 87–8, 103–6
horizontalisation 81–2
human relationships *see* relationships; social dimension
human worth 63
humanistic counselling 5–6
Husserl, E. 15–16, 28, 72–4

I-It/I-Thou 21, 76–7
identity *see* personal dimension; self
inauthenticity *see* authenticity
infinite 14, 38, 50
intentionality 27–31

Jaspers, K. 85

Kant, I. 66
Kierkegaard, S. 14, 20, 37–41, 103; paradoxes 45; self 50; stages of life 66–7
knowledge 7–8

lack 42
language 96
limit situations 85
listening 8–9, 80
literature 12
living 8, 13–14, 46–7, 65–8
logotherapy 126–8
love 97

Macaro, A. 68
Marcel, G. 113
May, R. 89, 113, 115

meaning 2, 13, 57–60, 104–6, 125–9
Merleau-Ponty, M. 16, 30, 34–5, 45–6, 113
Minkowski, E. 25
Mitsein see being-with
Mitwelt see social dimension
moods *see* emotions
morality 65–6, 105 *see also* values
Mulhall, S. 19–20, 24–5
Mullen, J. D. 38

natural environment 91
necessity 38, 50, 117
Nietzsche, F. 14, 20, 50–1, 67, 113

original project 58–9, 104
others *see* relationships; social dimension

paradoxes 45–7, 93, 117–20
paradoxical intention 127
person-centred counselling 5–6
personal dimension 49–52, 89, 99–102
phenomenological reduction 73
phenomenology 15–16, 28, 71–4
philosophy 5–9, 11–14; ancient philosophy 6–8, 45, 65, 68; Buber 21, 76–7, 103; Frankl 59–60, 104, 125–8; Merleau-Ponty 16, 30, 34–5, 45–6, 113; Nietzsche 14, 20, 50–1, 67, 113; phenomenology 15–16, 28, 71–4 *see also* Heidegger; Kierkegaard; Sartre
physical dimension 89, 91–4, 113–16
Plato 45, 65
pleasure 66
possibility 38, 50, 133
psychoanalysis 5
purpose *see* meaning

reduction 73–4
reflection 68
relationships 19–22 *see also* social dimension
repression 114–15
responsibility 13, 35, 127

Sartre, J.-P. 13–14, 95, 113; anxiety 37; being-for-others 20–1; competition and collaboration 22; emotions 197; freedom 34; intentionality 29–30; original project 58–9; self 49, 51–2; values 61–2
Schneider, K. J. 115
self 49–52, 99–102 *see also* authenticity; personal dimension
social dimension 5, 19–22, 89, 95–7
Socrates 6–7, 45, 65
Socratic dialogue 128
spiritual dimension 89, 103–6 *see also* holism
Stoicism 66
Strasser, F. 107
strength 101

taking stock 83–5
talents 84–5
Tarnas, R. 13
temporal 38–9, 50
temporality 24–6
tensions *see* paradoxes
the-They 20, 53–4
therapeutic relationship 5–6, 75–7

thrownness 17–18, 24
Tillich, P. 52, 58, 104
time 23–6, 38
transcendental reduction 74
truth 7

Überwelt see spiritual dimension
Umwelt see physical dimension

values 61–3, 84, 103–6, 108–10, 121–4
von Uexküll, J. 88

Warnock, M. 13, 16
well-lived life *see* living

Yalom, I. D. 46, 58

For Product Safety Concerns and Information please contact our EU representative GPSR@taylorandfrancis.com Taylor & Francis Verlag GmbH, Kaufingerstraße 24, 80331 München, Germany

Batch number: 10725861

Printed by Printforce, the Netherlands